To Jane

With Love

JcNeil

December 1992

A
Christmas
Housewarming

All proceeds received by
Habitat for Humanity in Atlanta
from the sale of this book will be used to build
houses for low-income families.
On behalf of the sixty families
on our waiting list, thank you in advance
for purchasing this book.

A
Christmas
Housewarming

Edited by Gene Stelten

Preface by Jimmy Carter

Peachtree Publishers
Atlanta

> To Mother and Dad, who taught me that
> Duty is Joy;
> To Jeannie, the greatest Joy that ever
> came into my life;
> To Jim, Sue, Lynn, Nancy, John and Bill,
> my ultimate blessings from God.

Published by
PEACHTREE PUBLISHERS, LTD.
494 Armour Circle, NE
Atlanta, Georgia 30324

Lovejoy Plantation Cookbook by Betty Talmadge.
Published by Peachtree Publishers, Atlanta, GA.
Reprinted with permission from the publisher.

Cover illustration donated by Leland Burke
Book design donated by Joan Body
Cover production donated by Atlanta Color Concepts
Illustrations donated by Georgia artists

Manufactured in the United States of America

10 9 8 7 6 5 4 3 2 1

Library of Congress Cataloging-in-Publication Data

A Christmas Housewarming/edited by Gene Stelten.
        p.   cm.
    ISBN 1-56145-065-0 : $12.95
    1. Christmas. 2. Christmas--Georgia. 3. Habitat for
Humanity in Atlanta, Inc.   I. Stelten, Gene.
GT498.C523 1992
394.2'68282'09758--dc20   92-26187
                                               CIP

Greeting

*May love go out
to all the world
in this joyous holiday season
and in the New Year.*

Peace and Blessings,

Andrew Young

ILLUSTRATION BY BETSY KOOLS

Preface

Nothing could better represent the spirit of Christmas than a book like this, filled with reminiscences of well-known people about their own seasonal joy and dedicated to the Habitat program of providing for God's people in need.

One of the greatest accomplishments of Habitat is to bring the problem of the homeless to the consciousness, and the conscience, of the people on earth. Habitat demonstrates that, first of all, we have a serious housing problem, and secondly, it's not a hopeless problem— something can be done about it.

In our work with Habitat, Rosalynn and I have learned more about the needy than I ever did as a governor, as a candidate, or as a president. The sacrifice I thought I would be making turned out to be one of the greatest blessings of my life.

I don't know of any organization that more vividly demonstrates love in action than Habitat for Humanity.

Jimmy Carter

Introduction

"The best Christmas we can remember was waking up in our brand-new Habitat house." So say Terina and Favous Horton, who moved from a one-bedroom apartment to their new three-bedroom Habitat house in 1990.

"The best Christmas was seeing our children come out of their own bedrooms, walking down that hall to our brand-new living room filled with all that new furniture and toys. Just seeing the look on their faces made me want to jump for joy."

"Christmas 1988 brought a new belief in ourselves," says Ossia Whitehead. "That was the year Calvin and I brought our two daughters and two sons to live in our new Habitat house. It was a new beginning for the Whitehead family."

For a low-income family, a Habitat house represents a new and more stable lifestyle. These families tell us about an increase in self-esteem. A place for the kids to do their homework. Better grades. Staying in school. Less chance for drugs. Families staying together.

Is it possible that a home can mean that much to a family? Don't take my word for it. Listen to a few Habitat families tell of their own Christmas memories on the following pages. You'll find their heartwarming stories interspersed with those of many prominent people in business, government, religion, sports, entertainment, education, the arts, and the media.

Every Habitat house is built by volunteers working side by side with the family who will live in the house. The family then buys the house from Habitat on a no-interest mortgage, and the payments are recycled to help finance another house.

It's like a living endowment. And when you purchase this book, part of the purchase price helps build a house. And then another. And another.

So please accept a sincere "Thank You" for becoming a part of this program, which is now operating in all fifty states!

If you would like to become more involved in this rewarding activity, please see the "Opportunities" page near the back of this collection.

I hope these Christmas memories will bring you the same enjoyment they brought to me in collecting them. It is my sincere wish that this collection will help you to have an especially happy holiday.

—G.S.
Reynoldstown
Atlanta, Georgia

Acknowledgments

Heartfelt gratitude goes to everyone who contributed a memento to this book, for lending your name and giving of your valuable time to help build homes for low-income families;

to everyone who contributed illustrations for this book, for donating your time and talent to the Habitat program;

to Joan Body, for contributing many hours of graphic design, illustration coordination, and computer entry;

to Habitat homeowners, for making the Habitat program work;

to Jimmy Carter, for his outstanding support of Habitat for many years;

to the Habitat for Humanity in Atlanta Board of Directors, for approving the idea and providing constant support and motivation;

to my wife Jeannie, for help in conceptualizing this project, communicating with contributors, and transcribing mementos, and—and—and—all along the way;

to Betty Boyce, a best friend, for ideas and interest and contacting prominent Georgians;

to Lynn Merrill, Jackie Goodman, Willie Hinton, Hal Clements, Bill Pendleton, Bill Earnest, Mary Alice Alexander, Bob Eskew, Janis Ware, Bill Adams, Mary Line, Alexandra Pieper-Jones, and Don Millen for help in contacting contributors to this volume;

to the gang at Peachtree Publishers, for believing in the project, and for working patiently with me to make this book a reality.

In Appreciation . . .

. . . to the following generous people for contributing to this project:

Christmas
Is
a
Family
Time

Celestine Sibley

In the days of my childhood Christmas was a scanty celebration for many country people. We had some strict puritanical neighbors who regarded it as the early Puritan settlers had—a pagan festival. The Ryans, on the other hand, were happy Irish settlers who believed in celebrating everything, especially the birthday of Jesus. But the year I remember best they weren't celebrating.

Grandpa Ryan, a white-bearded giant of a man, played Santa Claus at all the school and church parties, but not that year. He had pneumonia and was near death.

Pneumonia was a fearful illness in that day. It necessitated the stringent measure of calling the doctor to come all the way out from town over twenty miles of nearly impassable roads in winter's worst weather.

It called for all the relatives and neighbors to gather to be what help they could with firewood and food and coffee and steam kettles and poultices and even a drop of whiskey from the neighborhood shinny maker. Children with no place else to go and nobody to keep an eye on them also went and hung around the front porch and the barn, waiting with everybody else for word on the passing of The Crisis, which was the moment when they would know if Grandpa Ryan lived or died.

We were a grubby company sitting on the front steps that Christmas Eve, and I was sleepy and chilly and disgruntled because it

4

seemed that my parents, said to be "good hands at sick nussing," were needed in the sickroom. I wanted to go home and look at our Christmas tree and hang my stocking by the living room fireplace. I wanted to hear my mother play "Silent Night" on the piano.

"What you gon' get for Christmas?" I asked my two friends Ellie and May Ryan . . . . They looked vague.

May, the oldest, looked over her shoulder toward her grandpa's room.

"I don't want no things," she said haltingly. "Just grandpa."

"Yeah, grandpa," said Ellie.

It was my first intimation that a person might be more valuable than things.

Grandpa Ryan, sure, all of us children loved him. Could it be he would die this Christmas Eve?

It stunned me, and several other children on the top step stirred restlessly. The long wait dragged on. There were no Christmas lights, no tree or stocking in the Ryans' house, but sometime after midnight the girls' mother came out to the steps and gathered the children in her arms.

"He's gon' live, young'uns," she said. "Grandpa has passed The Crisis!"

Their faces, weary and pinched with cold and anxiety, were suddenly the brightest, happiest, most Christmasy sight I ever saw.

Sandra Deer

I want to speak here of my grand-parent's house on Pike Street. That house has long since disappeared into the progress of Gwinnett County, but its sounds and smells and shadows live with a crisp vigor in my memory. Although we—my sister and I and our cousins —adored both our grandparents, in the nomen-clature of our extended family, the house was always"Mama Sims' house." And it was to Mama Sims' house that we journeyed like wise men each Christmas of my childhood.

It was a white frame, one-story house on the corner of Pike Street and a little dirt road called Honeysuckle Lane. It had a front and side veranda with cane rocking chairs, and a back porch with a washing machine and a table for eating watermelon, folding laundry, or doing million-piece jigsaw puzzles.

There were three bedrooms in that house, and one bathroom. Eleven children had grown up there. The big bedroom in the middle of the house belonged to Mama and Papa Sims. It contained the big heater where a fireplace had once been, a large framed picture of cows drinking from a creek, a photograph of the handsome son who had died in the Second World War, the radio and later the television. The front bedroom, the one next to the living room, was called the girls' room becuase it was the one my mother and her four sisters had at various times shared. It had two double beds and a dresser full of old jewelry, perfumes and powder boxes. It was in the girls' room, the coldest room in the house, that my parents, my sister and I slept when we came at Christmas.

It is the Christmas Eve I was six or seven I am remembering now. Climbing in between those cold, cold sheets. My sister and I giggling and cuddling close. We can't wait. We've asked for everything. We always did, knowing that Santa, in his wisdom, would choose the exact right presents, and maybe even something wonderful we hadn't known to ask for. But this year I have asked for something special. Something I want desperately. A Sparkle Plenty doll. Will Santa bring her? How long before he and his helpers will be in the living room, just on the other side of the door, carefully arranging presents and filling stockings. What if I can't go to sleep? Will he skip our house? But I do, because the next thing I know I open my eyes and it is morning. Christmas morning.

My heart is so huge I can't breathe. I know the room on the other side of the door has been transformed. Someone, Mama Sims or Papa Sims or Daddy, will have already built a fire, and the living room will be alive with skates, dolls, a music box with a ballerina, stockings full of oranges, nuts and Hershey Bars. And Sparkle Plenty. It waits. The room waits. Holding its breath. The house waits in silence, and in that moment before I wake my sister, something happens. The house is me. I breathe life from this house. I take my being from these plaster walls, these cold wooden floors, the fire burning in the fireplace in the living room. I have become who I will be.

Who we are is our grandmother's house. Thank you Mama and Papa Sims for the house on Pike Street. Thank you Habitat for Humanity for houses all over the world.

Tom Key

The Three Wise Women

As a five-year-old Birmingham boy in 1955, I thought, "As far as Christmas goes--I've seen it all." Hadn't I witnessed moving reindeer, snowmen, and Dickensian shoppers in the downtown Loveman's department store? That electrical miracle and decorating spectacle was, in itself, our period's special effect, equivalent in shock value to the Terminator oozing back and forth from liquid to flesh.

I had also sat on the lap of Santa Claus himself; gazed out the rear window of our car for hours as my parents drove my brother and me through the glittering and gaudy colored outdoor-light competitions erected in subdivision after endless subdivision; witnessed my family consume for holiday dinner what looked to be the entire produce, poultry, and bakery section of the Piggly Wiggly store; received the most lusted-after gun and holster set, adored by our neighborhood gang chiefly for its particularly shiny straps and handle (pearls and diamonds?); and finally, I had been allowed to stay up as late as I pleased to watch the likes of Danny Kaye, Bob Hope, and Lawrence Welk entertain along Christmas themes through our brand-new and, it seemed, 5,000-pound television set.

I hadn't even begun school and I was already burned out over the events scheduled to mark the birth of Christ. Therefore, when my parents told me we were going, this Christmas, to spend the day with my three great-aunts in

9

Bessemer, I was more than disappointed; I was grim. Does Bessemer even have electricity? The youngest of the aunts was in her seventies--how much food could they cook? How could they conceive, much less afford, a present even close to my child-masculine tastes?

Fortunately for me, in that era, I could not dialogue with my parents on a first-name basis to discuss options. If I had, I might have missed one of my greatest Christmas presents. Mary Alice and Rutherford may have leaned toward spoiling me, but they did know when it was time to shut up, get in the car, and go.

It was just that way I was whisked off, literally to the other side of the tracks, to be put before Aunt Patsy, Aunt Judith, and Aunt Sarah--for a whole day. I fell asleep on the hour journey (today it probably takes twelve minutes), and when I awoke, this is what I saw: an enormous house, not suburban and low-ceilinged like ours, but with multiple stories and tall walls and windows, treacherously high steps to the front door, flocks of birds fluttering and cooing and flying, and ferns that looked large enough to feed a brontosaurus.

Then, they appeared, at the top of the stairs: the aunts coming to greet us. They moved as though choreographed. They weren't speaking as much as they were singing, lilting, cooing like the birds. Were those crowns on their heads?

"Oh, Tommy!" "So, this is hour-ah Tommy!" "Merry Christmas, darling!" "We love you so much!" "You are so handsome--just like your sweet daddy!" "Come in!" "Come in!" "Do you know how much we love you?!"

This is the way it went all day. Words of adoration, moist cakes, hugs of encouragement, chunks of fudgy chocolate, wise and quick smiles, juicy turkey, contented silences, all came effortlessly to my family and me. Why this intoxicating good cheer? Had I made all *A*' s, mowed lawns, or read through the complete Bible? No. Christmas and showing up were the only evident requirements for basking in this day of affection.

Twenty-five years later, as a break from graduate school studies, I took a trip back by to look at the aunts' old house. They had died by the time I finished high school. It was a shock how different the home looked that winter. The steps were crumbling, the birds were just dirty pigeons in legions, the ferns were kudzu--the "crowns" on their heads must have been poor dye jobs leaving the hair purple or pink.

On that cold December day, I realized how poor these women had been. And yet, of all my relations, they were able to afford my most expensive and enduring Christmas present: undeserved, extravagant attention.

If I have ever felt the capacity to be generous, charitable, or keep the Christmas spirit throughout the year, isn't it because others, like the aunts, first gave these treasures to me? At five, I had not "seen it all." Indeed, all the trappings of Christmas became forever opaque in the glaring vision of those three aunts, not from the east or bearing gold, frankincense, and myrrh, but from Bessemer bearing love.

Jeff Hullinger

Christmas for the Hullinger family in Denver always meant my father's dreadful red sweater and his unbridled enthusiasm for anything associated with December 25th.

My father was an unforgettable, child-like character who could shoot baskets, hit softballs, throw footballs, jog, bowl, fish, play ping-pong, cards, and croquet with the best of any crazed group of twelve-year-olds at camp. When he wasn't playing sports he was watching them on television.

As Christmas approached, his whirl of activity only increased. Now, instead of encouraging all of us to go bowling or shoot baskets, he would trot out the dreadful red sweater and sing along with a stack of yuletide tunes, encourag-

ing my mother, sister and me to join in. We eventually would, but not without his hyperactive prodding.

If Macaulay Culkin has come to serve as the Christmas metaphor of the '90s with his *Home Alone* movie, my dad would serve as the same figure for the '60s and '70s.

In 1968, we all pitched in to buy this 37-year-old a new red bicycle for Christmas, so with his nine-year-old son and six-year-old daughter in tow, the Hullingers rode around the neighborhood for hours (what a sight that must have been!).

Red bicycle, dreadful red sweater, and Dad singing Nat King Cole tunes—that was a Christmas I remember.

My father died in 1990, but those memories are as vivid as the dreadful red sweater he wore in December.

SLowell

Fran Tarkenton

As told by his daughter Angela

My dad really gets into Christmas big time.

Like the Christmas when we were all very young. Dad was shopping at the mall. He came upon this very jolly and excessively rotund Santa who was roaming the stores and talking to all the kids.

A light bulb went off in Dad's head. He knew exactly what had to be done.

So he convinced this huge Santa to get into his car and brought him to our house.

You can imagine our surprise as Santa Claus came in the front door, loaded down with presents and candy canes. The chimney hadn't been invented that could hold this guy.

We were bug-eyed with joy and excitement.

And the happiest kid on the block was Dad!

ILLUSTRATION BY LINDA MITCHELL

Leah Sears-Collins

My father was a hard-working, tough-minded army colonel who always carried himself with an air of certainty and authority that had nothing whatsoever to do with wealth or power, and everything to do with good character and strong faith. My father was the type of man who could not, and would not, accept second best in anything. Therefore, he was a very successful man.

While my father and mother (a school teacher) worked very hard to provide their three children with a bountiful Christmas, my dad often frowned on the conspicuous consumption and the lavish gift giving. It was unfamiliar and not quite right to a man who grew up with fourteen brothers and sisters in relatively modest circumstances during the Depression. I still remember Daddy's uncomfortable glances (he was too ill at ease to stop and stare) at the brightly packaged abundance which always began to grow beneath our Christmas tree a few weeks before Christmas. "All I really have to give you is good solid moral values and principles," he told me one Christmas when he was again taking in what he could of the sight of unopened gifts spread around the living room floor. "The only gift I want from you is for you to live by those principles and to pass them on," he added.

Just weeks before Christmas in 1989 I watched him leave this life. November 19, 1989, was the saddest day of my life. There would be no more special moments with my father, no more Christmases, no more gifts, I thought.

During the many Christmases since, however, I have had a chance to reflect on my loss. I now realize how completely my father enriched my life by his example. And I feel blessed that my father gave me a gift that will last forever when he showed me how a man should live his life. And I will pass those lessons on.

ILLUSTRATION BY BETSY KOOLS

Ray Goff

The Christmas that stands out most in my mind would have to be Christmas of 1990. I will never forget it, for I was coming off one of the most disappointing football seasons that we had ever had here at the University of Georgia. We had been to ten straight Bowl games, and there were a lot of disappointed Georgia fans, including myself. However, this gave me the opportunity to go home for Christmas.

I had not been home for Christmas in twelve years. I was able to spend that time with my mom, my dad, my wife and daughters, my younger brother, and my sister and her family. As I spent time in Moultrie that Christmas, little did I know that it would be our last Christmas together--in February of 1991 I lost my father.

I look back now and realize that the Lord works in mysterious ways. Even though I don't feel that this was the reason we had a losing season, I believe it's a miracle the way God can take something bad, like the kind of football season we had, and turn it into something positive. He allowed me to spend that extra time at home with me not realizing it would be my last Christmas I would ever spend with my father.

After that losing season, I will never forget that my dad told me we would go eight and three the next season. Fortunately for us, we did go eight and three, and an even greater opportunity we had was to go to a Bowl game, win, and be nine and three.

On the following Christmas, even though we had a tremendous amount of success athletically, there was still a big void left in my life at Christmas time. This was a very tough Christmas for me personally because it was the first one we as a family had ever experienced without my father, who was obviously the leader of our house.

It all goes to show that there are more important things in life than football and athletics. God has blessed us all with a mother and a father, and we need to appreciate, understand, and love them. We should never be ashamed to tell anyone that we love them because there will come a time in our life when, unfortunately, they won't be there--and we'll never have the opportunity ever again to sit down and look in their eyes and tell them how much we love them.

I think these were the best and the toughest Christmases that I have ever experienced, and as I reflect on these experiences, I see the love that God has for all of us; that he gave his son, Jesus Christ, to die for each and every one of us, because of that love. That is what makes Christmas to me.

Bo Emerson

Christmas Bear

Mama didn't know whether to tell me. Papa was going to dress like Santa Claus and visit my kindergarten class in Atlanta's Spring Street School, to hand out candy canes and bellow good cheer. His laugh, a reverberating roar of high spirits, was perfect for the part.

They thought I might be frightened by the charade—"Why is Papa in a red suit?"— so they decided to warn me. "Papa's going to pretend," Mama explained. "He's helping Santa Claus."

But when Papa, clad in a cotton-wool beard, strode into Miss Joyce's classroom and roared glad tidings, I forgot my preparation. I looked in my father's face and saw Father Christmas. When I sat on his red velvet lap, I thought deeply before I revealed what I really wanted. A bear.

This was news to Santa Claus. Christmas morning came, and under the tree was a sleepy-eyed bear as tall as me. Mama thought the bear was too big, but I was in heaven. Somehow the sleepy bear managed to survive my affections, and is now a beloved companion of my four-year-old daughter, Molly.

ROYAL

ILLUSTRATION BY SUZANNE ROYAL

Mattie Lou O'Kelley

Papa's Trunk

Christmas! That magic word for all the world, especially children. And this was going to be a very special time for my little brother and me.

The kitchen was smelling all spicy and mysterious, the fire was roaring up the kitchen fireplace, defying Santa Claus's visit that night, my older sisters were floating through the house like beautiful butterflies, and all over the house things just seemed to be happening, as if by some strange unseen power.

Johnnie and I wondered how Santa Claus was going to get down the chimney that night with such a glorious, roaring fire booming up the only entrance to the house's insides that the poor man had? But nobody had time to answer our questions.

Johnnie and I had already hung up our stockings on last year's nails, and we could hardly wait. Mama had promised this year to show me and Johnnie the insides of the big old trunk that sat in the long hall. Always it had been full of secrets for us, and sometimes we would sneak up to the trunk, which was never locked, wondering what was in it. But Mama would always see us and tell us not to dare touch it. We had learned long ago to mind our mother, who was a good hand with a peachtree switch.

But this year Mama had said that learning the secret of the trunk would be our Christmas present, as Santa was short-handed this year, whatever that meant.

All year Mama had said there would be no turkey this Christmas, as we needed the money for other things, like school shoes and stockings, and Gertrude, the sick one, had to have medicine so she could get well. But now she was dressing one of her prized turkeys for tomorrow, and we had to wait till she finished before opening the trunk.

At last we stood in awe, our mouths hanging open, waiting in silent wonder as the heavy lid was raised. There, first and foremost, was the huge black hat our father had purchased over a year before and never worn, saying it was his "Sunday" hat. Then some strange-looking papers our mother said were our father's business papers, then some more "Sunday" clothes that belonged to our father and that he had never worn, saying he never had time to wear them because he had to work on his farm to support his family of a wife and eight children.

We were thrilled to solve the mystery of the trunk, and as the afternoon wore on, we forgot about Santa Claus's visit. The snow was falling outside, the turkey was in the oven, and Papa got down on his all-fours to "play bear" with us. That was a very happy Christmas.

Pam Martin

One Christmas Eve my little sister Joanne and I hung our stockings, left cookies for Santa, and were packed off to bed. As Mom and Dad had quite a bit of work to do, they decided to warn us that Santa wouldn't come if we didn't go to sleep. But the hours ticked by and we were still wide awake.

Then we heard an incredible sound: sleigh bells and stomping on our roof! Joanne and I were so shocked we closed our eyes and were fast asleep in seconds.

Years later I found out that it wasn't reindeer, but Dad, who had climbed up on the roof. I'll always carry with me the mental picture of him stamping his feet in the cold, shaking those jingle bells, waiting for his daughters to finally go to sleep.

My hope is that each year, more of our children will go to sleep on Christmas Eve and every day of the year with a fine roof over their heads, and the possibility of sleigh bells in the air.

Bobby Rowan

I was the middle child in a family of nine children raised on a mule farm. In 1944, my three older brothers were away in the war. Ventan was in Japan, Charles was flying missions over Germany. My older brother Tom was in the Navy on the *U.S.S. Vulcan*, a repair ship, but censorship prevented Tom from letting us know where he was located.

It was a bad crop year and everyone knew Christmas would be sparse. A few days before Christmas, a letter was received from brother Tom. On top of the letterhead were the words "anchored in waters off Iceland." The censor had missed it and we knew for the first time where Tom was located. Daddy got out the world map and determined Iceland was outside the range of the war threat.

Daddy, a devout Christian, declared it was a Christmas present from God to a family that loves, on a bad crop year. The gift was a feeling that brother Tom was safe.

We might have gotten some material things, I don't remember, but 1944 was and still is the greatest Christmas gift I remember.

Mary Alice Alexander

Christmas traditions in many families are quite involved.

Not so in mine. Exception was the tradition in my family. My mother believed that change was the order of the season.

Every year the Christmas tree was in a different room in our house, which meant that some years it was in various bedrooms! Imagine Christmas morning with everyone charging into your room and jumping on the bed. It was wonderful, wacky fun.

After my brother and I got older and he was away for long and anxious years serving two tours of duty in Vietnam as a Navy pilot, he was at last coming home. It was July of 1971.

Family heads were together busily organizing a "special homecoming" for his first day home. His wife and son helped by being at the airport alone to greet him. If he wondered where the rest of his family was, he was probably too happy to hold and kiss his own little family to think about it.

That year, in July, the Christmas tree was in his old room and we made up for all those without him.

Johnny Beckman

When I was a youngster my big brother was my hero. He was seven years older than I was, but he never treated me like a "little brother." He let me follow him around—he took care of me.

I remember one Christmas when I wanted a bicycle more than anything else in the world. I had heard my parents talking about "the Depression" and "hard times" and I knew that there were skimpy meals on the table, so there really wasn't much hope for me getting a bicycle—my brother didn't even have one. But, he told me to go ahead and write a letter to Santa and we'd see what happened.

That Christmas Eve was the longest night of my life. Before dawn I sneaked out of the bed my brother and I shared and crept into the living room. And there by the Christmas tree stood a beautiful red and gold and shiny Western Flyer bicycle. I was so excited I couldn't wait . I shook my brother out of bed and we took the bike out in the cold morning air and he helped me learn to ride it, running along beside me, holding me up, keeping me from falling. We were laughing and shouting—God, how I loved that bike!

It wasn't until many years later that I learned my brother, who was at the time working after school and on weekends, had taken an extra job to make money so that Santa could bring me a bicycle.

Not long after that wonderful Christmas

my brother volunteered to go off and fight for
America in World War II. He never came back.
But I still think about him a lot, especially
at Christmas time. And I'll never forget that
beautiful bicycle.

Christmas
Is
for
Children

Glenda Hatchett Johnson

The miracle of Christmas was never so meaningful as the Christmas that immediately followed the birth of my first child. In all my life I had never known the pure joy of the experience of his birth. His life, then and now, continues to be a miraculous blessing in our lives.

I truly believe that in our children lies hope and strength for all of our tomorrows.

As I reflect upon that Christmas morning when I held that precious infant in my arms, I am reminded of God's abundant blessings, the essence of Christmas and the divine miracle of life.

The joy and peace of that Christmas morning is my prayer for all children and all parents throughout the world.

ILLUSTRATION BY LISA MATRUNDOLA

George (Buddy) Darden

The first of the best and most memorable Christmases of my life was in 1971, when my wife Lillian and I brought our week-old daughter Christy home from the hospital on Christmas Eve.

All our Christmases with Christy, and later her brother George, have been wonderful and memorable, but there was something very special about that first one. We had our own tiny babe to hold as we joined the worldwide celebration of the birth of another babe in a manger in faraway Bethlehem.

We had not expected our baby until January, so we were doubly blessed to have her with us for Christmas, hale and hearty, as, thankfully, her mother was also.

Christy's participation in our Christmas festivities has changed as the years have gone by, from that wee, helpless stranger we cherished so well, through years of tacky tree trimming thanks to questionable assistance from her and George, past the Santa years to the present, when we have two beautiful, intelligent, mature children who brighten our lives on Christmas and every other day.

Glenn (Doc) Rivers

Christmas has always been special for me. My family was never closer than on Christmas morning. Each Christmas I would wake up early to see what Santa had left under the tree. I knew he had come because the cookies and milk I left for him were gone. My parents went to great lengths to protect that myth for as long as they could.

Under the tree were many gifts for my brother and me, but very few for mom and dad. I often wondered why they didn't get more. I assumed Christmas was for kids, but my parents seemed to enjoy it just as much as we did.

On July 27, 1987, my first child was born, Jeremiah Jordan Rivers. On his first Christmas I understood why my parents enjoyed Christmas so much. Watching him go from gift to gift brought a joy to me that I had never experienced.

My mom always said "it's better to give than to receive." Christmas is the birthday of the One who always gave. Looking at the smile on Jeremiah's face, I thought my mom was right.

Kenny & Marianne Rogers

We think our most memorable Christmas was when our son, Christopher, was five. At last, he was old enough to appreciate the meaning of Christmas and the excitement it brings.

Christopher woke us up early that morning. He eagerly explained that Santa's milk, cookies and letter were gone, and that he had left some gifts.

As Christopher waited impatiently, we hurried out of bed and went to the Christmas tree together. We will never forget the awe and excitement that lit up Christopher's shining face as he approached the twinkling tree, with all the gaily wrapped gifts beneath it. The pleasure of watching him will always stand out in our minds.

Amidst this joy and excitement, I asked Christopher what he thought the best thing about Christmas was, thinking he would say the presents. He looked at me and said, "The best thing is that it's Jesus's birthday and he came to save us." We were happy that he understood this at such an early age.

Skip Caray

As a child at Christmas I still remember some "reindeer bells" that my uncle Ellsworth always had. We celebrated the gift-giving portion of the holiday on Christmas Eve and nobody was allowed near the tree until those bells were heard indicating that Santa had departed from our house. I can shut my eyes today and hear those bells as clearly now as I did then.

As a teenager I was fortunate enough to sing in the high school choir, and I still remember the words to all the carols we sang. I've often wished I had stayed with the singing but the traveling and the career got in the way and I wasn't smart enough to make the time.

As a "grown-up" (the older I get the more I realize there is no such thing) I have been blessed with a second family. Now, at age fifty-two, I have a ten-year-old son and I've gotten to see the Christmas season through his eyes despite my vintage years. I think this third part has been the best of all. I appreciate things so much more now than with my first batch of kids when I was younger.

Rawson & Margaret Haverty

It was the Christmas of 1957—frankly, not one of our best. Margaret had just brought us our fourth child. It had been a particularly difficult delivery, and she was still very weak. My father fell ill and broke his hip, and his physician, Dr. Glenville Giddings, told me just before Christmas that my father had developed Parkinson's disease. I remember also that I bought for my youngest son a toy filling station from Sears Roebuck. After the kids had gotten to bed, about ten o'clock, I opened up the gift to get it ready, and the instructions said, "Start early. This takes a long time." After getting tab 52a into slot 52b and so on, I got the present in shape for Christmas by about 2:30 in the morning.

Nevertheless, the picture remains in my mind of our children coming down the stairs on Christmas morning. They looked like little angels to us, and when the kids came down and found out that Santa Claus really had arrived, Christmas day turned out, as always, a happy time.

Ernest F. Boyce

From my earliest memories in Milton, Massachusetts, Christmas has been synonymous with the faces of children, young and old, as they prepare to give and to receive. I can still see the rapturous expressions on the faces of my sister and brother as we came downstairs on Christmas morning to the only gifts the Depression could muster—stockings filled with oranges, apples, raisins, nuts and candy.

Years later I recognized these same smiles on the faces of my children and grandchildren on Christmas morning. Betty and I have enjoyed twenty-seven Christmases together in Atlanta, each with a special feeling or memory. We often recall our two-year-old who, in the excitement of Christmas Eve, simply toppled into the tree, and grabbing it for support, brought all twelve feet of it down on top of him. As we dashed in from the kitchen all we could see of our son was his curly head poking through the tinseled branches, tears streaming down his cheeks because now, with no tree, Santa Claus would not come to our house.

Christmas at Colonial Stores was always filled with giving. I was touched by the way my associates looked out for those in need at the holidays. And, occasionally, when I had the privilege of playing Santa Claus to certain Colonial families, I shall never forget their expressions of gratitude, no matter how small the gesture.

Smiles and loving looks are the joyful memories of Christmas for me.

Eldrin Bell

My oldest daughter, Terry, was three or four years old at the time. It was Christmas season, and we were having the first snow fall she had ever seen.

So naturally, we went for a walk in the snow. Terry walked right behind me.

"Look, Daddy, I'm stepping in your steps."

Her words hit me right in the heart and brought tears to my eyes. I realized that she would be "stepping in my steps" many times during her life.

So I picked her up in my arms, held her close, and said to her, "What a wonderful Christmas present."

Another reason to walk straight!

ILLUSTRATION BY MIKKI FORD

Jill Becker

Growing up with my family in St. Louis, I have many wonderful memories of Christmas. It was a magical time for a young child, with cookies and candies, the Christmas tree, relatives visiting, big dinners in the dining room!

But while many good times come to mind when I think back, I must admit that no Christmas has been more special to me than the Christmas just past . . . the Christmas of 1991.

My husband, John, and I have two wonderful children, Gregory and Matthew. Two years ago, Matt, our youngest, was diagnosed with cancer. He had just turned three at the time. He had a massive tumor in his chest. It was a frightening time for us, as were the eighteen months of chemotherapy he underwent. But this story has a happy ending. Matthew is free of cancer, he's finished his chemotherapy and seems well on his way to living a happy, healthy life.

That brings me to this Christmas. The

holiday so full of family and love and what life is really all about, truly brought home how much God has blessed our family. He has given us each other, and our bout with illness has taught us to try to keep that Christmas spirit in the family year-round. It was a magical Christmas, a blessed Christmas, the most memorable of my life . . . and I'm looking forward to many, many more with my beautiful, healthy family.

Dan Sweat

I never met a Christmas I didn't like.

Whether it was growing up as a child and anticipating the arrival of Santa, or experiencing the love of Christ and watching my children bask in the glow of the season, Christmas has always been a time of rejoicing.

But the best Christmas I have ever had was the one just past—1991.

Because Sydney was there!

Sydney is our four-year-old granddaughter and our heart's delight.

Last Labor Day, while visiting with her grandmother, Tally, and me, Sydney developed a fever and we had to return her to her parents, Steve and Ruthie, at their home in Tucker.

She was admitted to Egleston Children's Hospital and was diagnosed as having a form of cancer rare in children. After two of the most difficult months in the lives of all our family, Sydney was released from Egleston in time to share in the Christmas celebration. Although she was weak and exhausted from her hospital stay and from painful chemotherapy treatments she must take, her spirit and her love made Christmas 1991 the best ever.

Bobby Ross

I think that in any person's life Christmas is a very special time, and almost every Christmas has had very fond memories for me. I think it took until the age of fifty-three before I had my strongest appreciation of what was a great Christmas. That particular Christmas occurred when my son Chris and his wife DiAnne and their two children, Kimberly and Rebecca, visited us. This Christmas was so special because little Rebecca, who was at this time our thirteen-month-old granddaughter, had been through so much. Rebecca had been born with serious heart defects and had actually gone through a transplant operation at the age of eight weeks. She was doing extremely well and making a very fine recovery during this period of time. We had gone through so much with her during the many operations and the many concerns over whether she would survive the operation or the heart transplant. This was to be our first Christmas together with young Rebecca.

Of course they arrived and of course we had what was to me the finest Christmas we have ever had. This was the first Christmas for my wife and myself as grandparents and it meant an awful lot to us to have the opportunity to share some wonderful moments, not only with our son and his wife and our other children, but also, for the first time, with our two grandchildren. It was particularly special to have Rebecca there as part of our family. We had a family portrait taken the day before Christmas and it was one of the more memorable days of my entire life. The following morning we awakened and I can recall sitting and holding young Rebecca on my lap while everyone else opened Christmas gifts. It was a very special moment to me. Rebecca was a wonderful child and had a great smile, and when you looked at her she was so appreciative and so smiling and loving.

Christmas ended, as all do, and my son and his wife returned. On the following March 4th, we received a phone call from my son, who indicated to us that Rebecca was being rushed to the hospital in a life-saving attempt. They never got to the hospital in the sense that Rebecca suffered a heart rejection and died. Obviously, it was not an easy thing for us to go through as a family, but we have our God and our family relationships to help us get through it.

I still have that picture and have it sitting very proudly behind my desk in my office. She was a special child and our memories of her will always linger, but I think the thing I will remember most in my entire life is that Christmas with Rebecca.

ILLUSTRATION BY MARK CORT

Ernie Johnson

Michael is a blond three-year-old. The first two and a half years of his life were spent in an iron crib. He was warehoused with other abandoned babies in a foul-smelling orphanage in Romania.

After two months of legal wrangling, Michael and his new mom arrived in Atlanta. Through adoption, our son Ernie and his wife Cheryl had rescued this little guy, who couldn't talk and was unable to walk due to a club foot.

Braces miraculously straightened his foot. But prayers and love from his parents, brother Eric, sister Maggie and all his new relatives helped make the Christmas of 1991 our greatest. Michael not only experienced the excitement of seeing his first Christmas tree, meeting Santa Claus, and opening a present— but on this joyous religious celebration, he walked by himself for the first time.

ILLUSTRATION BY JILL DUBIN

47

Sharon Sheats

It was my pleasure to be a part of the work crew from Southern Bell. We helped Priscilla Knight and her family build their new Habitat house. It was fun painting and caulking and scraping paint as part of the cleanup crew.

Priscilla has written a heartwarming Christmas memento for this book, thanking the Habitat people for being there when she needed them. This reminds me of a time when I desperately needed help, too.

It was Christmas of 1987. Nine years earlier, my daughter had been born with a congenital heart defect. She had been through numerous surgeries since the age of three months.

Our doctor recommended a heart transplant. But I was filled with mixed emotions. I dreaded putting my child through another major operation. And I knew that some child would have to die so that my child could live. Perhaps the solution was to rely on the medication. But I knew that this would cause deterioration of her other organs.

It was a difficult decision to put her on the list for a heart transplant. But we did it.

Around Halloween of 1987 she became sick. By Thanksgiving she was weak. Her heart was beating but not doing anything. Finally, on Christmas Eve, my radio pager signaled me that a heart was available. A child in Pennsylvania had been in an auto accident.

Today that child's heart beats in my daughter's body. And she's doing fantastic.

John Stone

Prematurity
"Life can only be
understood backwards,
but it must be lived
forwards."
—Søren Kierkegaard

And so it came to pass, some twenty years ago, that I waited, sweating in December, looking out over Atlanta from the sixteenth floor of Grady Memorial Hospital. My red-and-white-trimmed suit was scratchy, but my rumpled red hat flopped just right (I hoped). The dense white make-believe beard completely covered my own short salt-and-pepper one.

Then, with no fanfare, I was being ushered into an adjacent large room filled with excited children and parents. I'd been roped into playing Santa by a colleague, the director of the neonatal unit at Grady Hospital. All the children there were certified "graduates" of the unit, and this Christmas party was an annual reunion. I could imagine what these kids must have looked like as patients: we've all seen, on television, their metaphorical brothers and sisters--two-pounders whose thin limbs flail, whose soft rib cages seem to crumple in and out with each breath through their newly discovered lungs. Milling around me were medical school faculty and students greeting former patients; few suspected that under the Santa suit was one of their own colleagues, his considerable paunch enhanced by a strategically placed pillow.

When I was a medical student, I remember trying to understand why such tiny newborns have such large medical problems, why they often die. Once, a pediatrician gave me a one-word explanation: "Prematurity," he said, trying to sound wiser than he was. I'm happy to say that over the decades since I was a junior medical student, neonatal medicine has come a long way--and so have the children.

Back now in my Santa get-up, I pressed through the crowd, giving my arrival my thespian best. ("Look, Cindy, there's Santa! Can you wave at Santa?") I was guided to a chair in the center of the room and, warily, took a seat. Then, in a stream, the children came—from six pounds to sixty—and sat, each in turn, on my lap. Those old enough to talk did so with no prompting, chattering on about their hopes and dreams for the upcoming holidays—and for life.

I remember best a set of twins, boys about four years old, spiffy in their identical plaid suits. They sat, in genetic triumph, one on each of my knees. They giggled, squirmed, and tugged at my beard. Their mother told me that they weren't exactly equal at birth. "Edward was small," she said, "but Eugene was teeny. We didn't know whether he'd make it." I looked hard at the twins; they were robust perfect doubles. Clearly Eugene had caught up. I gave each a long hug as they hopped down.

I understand now why I remember those twins so well. Symbolically, they were my own two sons (not twins), one of whom was a couple of months premature himself and spent his own first mortal days in a plastic bassinette bathed in oxygen, sipping hospital syrups through his veins. But my wife and I had to shuttle anxiously between hospital and home for only ten days before our son was released, cured. Some of these parents had sweated it out for months.

Now, in memory, those twins are as surely Christmas as my own family. Over the years, as each Christmas Past has become Christmas Present, there have been many happy Christmases. But there was a sad one in December 1991, only a few months after the sudden death of my wife. No one loved Christmas more than she did. She was fifty-four years old. Her death was as terribly premature as any premature birth could be.

Nevertheless, again this December, in loss, I and my family will celebrate Christmas. We will do so, because life must be lived "forwards." I learned that fact indelibly, years ago, from those tiny graduates of the neonatal unit. And from their parents, all of whom had worried that their child might not live to see that first Christmas, let alone a succession of them. So this year and for however many Christmases are left to me, I will live forwards. St. Francis was right when he said, "Anticipation is the greater joy." One of the blessings of this holiday is the hope—the belief—that the most memorable Christmas of all could well be the next one.

Christmas
Across
the
Miles

David Chandley

Christmas is a time for families. I think of my grandmother's house, full of food, laughter and love. It is the season of sharing and of giving and of togetherness. I can appreciate what my family means to me. Back in 1982 I had the experience of spending Christmas morning alone: no family, no loved ones, not even a Christmas stocking. But I did this by choice.

As a student at the University of Georgia, I worked in the athletic department as a student trainer. I taped ankles, knees, tended to minor emergencies, provided a bridge between the athletes and the team physicians. If you recall the early 1980s, Georgia's football program was the best in the country and in December of 1982, we were preparing for our third straight trip to the Sugar Bowl in New Orleans.

Taking some 120 players, coaches, managers, trainers and support staff to a Bowl game for a week takes tremendous coordination. With the team due to leave Athens on December 26th, everything had to be set up in New Orleans beforehand.

Since my parents lived in Colorado and I hadn't met my wife yet, I volunteered to accompany team staff member Ray McEwen and his family to New Orleans three days before Christmas. We drove a Suburban which pulled a trailer containing all the team uniforms, training supplies and equipment.

The Sugar Bowl officials tried to make my Christmas a little less lonely. They had a tree in my hotel room, they took care of my meals, in elaborate New Orleans fashion. I even brought a few presents from home so I would have something to do on Christmas morning.

I awoke that Christmas morning, not to the sounds of children playing with their new toys, but to the silence of a party town, still fast asleep. I threw on a warm-up and hit the streets. The French Quarter was quiet, shops and restaurants and bars all closed up. Even the panhandlers were gone (I wondered where they were). As I walked along the river, and through Jackson Square, it saddened me to see drunks still lying in the alleys. For them it was not Christmas morning, it was just another day. Another day alone.

After an hour or so of observing and reflecting, I thanked God I was blessed. That Christmas morning I was alone . . . but by my choice. The experience would allow me to be forever grateful that I had a family, a family that I love and that loves me.

I hurried back to the hotel to call my parents and sister, then I opened my gifts. But even as I tore through the wrapping paper, I knew I had just received the most precious gift anyone could receive. It was learning what Christmas and family is all about.

Pete Van Wieren

A traditional family Christmas is the norm for the Van Wierens. But the Christmas I'll never forget stands in stark contrast to this.

I was assigned to televise an NBA game in Philadelphia on Christmas night, 1987.

Several minutes before our 8 P.M. airtime, Antoine Carr of the Atlanta Hawks shattered a glass backboard during warm-ups.

Steve Jones and I had to fill air-time for over an hour while repairs were made, then televise the game.

It was nearly midnight when we headed back to our downtown Philadelphia hotel. All attempts to find a spot for a post-game snack failed. Everything was closed, including room service.

As I sat in my room, munching some stale cheese and crackers from a hotel vending machine, I sensed how difficult it must be for those who spend Christmas away from their families or alone every year.

Tommy Nobis

The year was 1965 and I was proud to be chosen to play in the North versus South college all-star football game to be played on Christmas Day in Miami, Florida.

The festivities started the week before the game. Being a college boy from Texas, I had never experienced the special treatment extended to me during that week. There wasn't a dull moment to be had as I attended party after party—meeting new and attractive people wherever I turned.

I was having a great time—and— before I knew it, Christmas Eve had snuck up on me. There I sat in my hotel room realizing that this was the first Christmas I had ever spent away from home.

As exciting as the build-up to the game had been, the homesickness brought me back "down to earth" and made me realize the importance of this family holiday.

There is no place like home for the holidays—Amen, Brother!

Brendan Breault

When I was twelve my family was living in Atlanta. We flew up to Boston to spend the holidays with my relatives. We left Boston on Christmas Eve to drive up to Bangor, Maine, where my aunt and uncle live.

That year there was a terrible snow storm on I-95, the road from Boston to Bangor. I remember being very excited about Christmas, the gifts, playing in the snow with my cousins.

Because the snow was so intense the normal five-hour trip took nine hours. I'm sure my brother and sister and I drove my parents crazy during the drive. At one point along the way we stopped for gas and debated whether or not to finish the drive. When we finally arrived well after midnight, it was so wonderful to be with my family in a nice, warm home.

I don't remember what gift I got that year, but I learned the importance of family during the Christmas season.

ILLUSTRATION BY LOUISE BRITTON

Newt Gingrich

I will never forget the year Congress was in session until about forty-eight hours before Christmas. That was 1985. The first session of the 99th Congress ended about four in the morning, then we jumped in the car and drove back home to Carrollton.

We pulled into the driveway the night before Christmas Eve, totally exhausted from working up to the last minute and the long drive. But we got up the next morning, wandered around town, bought one of the last Christmas trees available, and did all of our Christmas shopping for the family during the day at the stores which were still open. At about five in the afternoon, in total exhaustion but also total relief, we stopped and put everything together.

And, frankly, as we rested and saw everybody on Christmas Day, there was a tremendous sense of relaxation and enjoyment. Luckily all the presents left in stores that we had bought turned out to be just the right ones. It had all been worth it as we celebrated a Carrollton Christmas after a long fall in Washington.

Furman Bisher

All of my Christmases as a child seem to run together. Warm, pleasant, plentiful but never extravagant, yea, anything but extravagant. The rewarding part of it was the giving. I'd save money from magazines I sold, lawns I mowed, blackberries I picked and sold and other such entrepreneurial ventures and invest in gifts I wanted my parents to have, and my brother and sisters.

The Christmas that stands out most in my life is not one I remember with pleasure. I was in Hawaii, an ensign in the Navy Air Corps, spending my first Christmas away from home. I went into Honolulu and sat in the telephone office much of the day waiting for my turn to call home.

There was a big fellow from Texas ahead of me, a civilian worker, and he was trying to call home, which was in Burkburnett. The conversation was comic, this big fellow trying to explain to the operator: "No, no," he said, "it ain't a feller. Burkburnett is a town. It's where I come from, ma'am."

"Denton" wasn't hard to understand or spell and I got through right away. I don't think I was ever so lonesome in my life, never felt such a yearning for home and fireside by the Christmas tree. What that Christmas taught me was how much home meant to me, and how much it meant to be home for Christmas, where the heart is, where the loved ones are.

Brenda Bynum

I've spent only one Christmas outside of Georgia in my whole life.

By 1971 I had been living in Manhattan for eight years but always headed home for the holidays with my husband, whose family lived here too, and then with our first son, whose grandparents were happy to show up at the airport no matter what time the low-cost night flight arrived. But in October of that year our second northern-born son arrived, and we decided to keep a quiet, restful Christmas in our own little New York nest. We assured our four-year-old that the same bountiful Santa who always visited him at two houses in Atlanta (one with a real chimney and the other with plenty of sleigh-landing room on the lawn) would adapt with no trouble to the small elevator that rose to our seventh-floor apartment.

My husband and I began to feel very grown-up about managing this grandest of celebrations all on our own. But by the week before the big day the twenty-four-hour baby-care blues, combined with the relentless northern winter, had me housebound and sick with flu. There was no tree, no Santa Claus hidden in the closet, no cookies baking, and no seats available on any flight south until January. My hard-working husband had a milder version of the same malaise as I, and we just managed to get from one day to the next, him at the job and me holding on at home.

He was finally off on Christmas Eve day. We spent the day taking turns baby-sitting and struggling out into the freezing city to get antibiotics from the doctor, food from the market, what toys and gifts we could find in the mom-and-pop shops on our block, a tree—then back to our apartment to collapse.

That weary Christmas Eve night we put our little ones to bed, noticing but not acknowledging the silent doubt in our oldest son's eyes. We spread our meager offerings from St. Nick under the tree and sat in the soft light, exhausted. We felt grateful for peace and warmth, but were nagged by the feeling that we really weren't quite grown-up enough to be in charge of such a major life event as Christmas all by ourselves. Why, oh why, we wondered, hadn't we gone home and let the experts handle it?

We slept at last, and in our dreams, we thought, we heard the pitter-patter of tiny reindeer hooves. . . . But no! What we really heard was the slip-slap of the plastic feet on a size 4 blanket-sleeper as its occupant ran down the hall toward the tree and then, in the dawn dimness, back down the hall toward our room.

As he slid around the corner we prepared ourselves for howls of disappointment, but instead Shakespeare's "bird of dawning" filled the room with light and song as our fuzzy, rumpled, snaggle-toothed and glowing little boy squeezed his new black-and-white Snoopy dog with the big red bow and caroled, "He'th came!" "He'th came!"

He came indeed, and we found ourselves able to keep a very fine Christmas—the four of us perched high in that city so far from the soft, pine-scented land we had always called home. That year we found out that Christmas comes anywhere you happen to be, and we have derived much faith and comfort from that notion over the years—even though, to tell the truth, we've never risked looking for it outside of Georgia again.

Don Farmer

In December of 1970 I was assigned by ABC News to go to Cairo, Egypt, to cover the ongoing Middle East struggle.

The assignment lasted through the Christmas holidays. There I was in a Muslim land, far from wife and children, facing a Christmas lacking in the kinds of traditions, decorations, music, and family that I enjoyed so much in other years.

After some hours of depression and moping, I decided to make something of this holiday where few people celebrated it.

So I went to the Giza pyramid and hired the famous camel jockey who rents out his camel, known as "Canada Dry," for rides to tourists there.

I hired the man and his beast for the entire day, took them into the city of Cairo and gave camel rides to a lot of the European kids whose families lived in the diplomatic and journalistic neighborhood.

It was fun for them—a different kind of Christmas on board a camel—and a great diversion for me.

Even now I still recall that Christmas; not the best ever, but my most unusual.

ILLUSTRATION BY WALT FLOYD

Bill Lewis

At this time we were living in North Carolina, but we had lived in the Rocky Mountain region for several years. Our son Gregg was attending the Air Force Academy in 1989 and instead of having him come to North Carolina, our family decided to join him for Christmas in the Rockies.

Our sons, Mark and Geoff, Mark's wife, Wendy, Sandy and I arrived in Denver several days before Christmas. We met Gregg and traveled to our small, cozy condominium. It was a winter wonderland, with crisp, cold air and mounds of snow and a buzz of activity.

On the day before Christmas, as our family returned from a day of skiing, the preparations began for our evening meal. During this time, conversation was about other Christmas holidays. We were having a wonderful time just being together, but we did miss our holiday tree, which was always decorated with memories of the past.

After dinner, Gregg and Geoff put on their coats and headed out the door for a walk, probably to avoid the after-dinner clean-up. An hour later they returned with a small tree about three feet tall. We found a container for the tree and placed it on the counter and began to decorate it.

Each person had to contribute something to the tree made from things we had with us. Gregg made a star for the top from aluminum foil. Geoff carefully hung Q-tips as though they were icicles. Wendy fashioned a garland by tearing newspaper strips and linking them together. Mark placed cotton balls on the branches to look like snow. Sandy added earrings and bracelets and I hung cookies and candy canes.

When we were finished, we all agreed it was beautiful. We ended our decorating by sitting around the tree singing our favorite Christmas carols. The last carol of the night was "Silent Night," which we sang as the soft white snow was falling. This was a very special family Christmas.

Dr. Charles B. Knapp

Over the years, the Knapp family has celebrated Christmas in different locations of the country as college, work, and job opportunities required movement from one city to another. Whether it was in Iowa, Texas, Washington, D.C., or Louisiana, the Christmas season has been special to my wife, Lynne, daughter, Amanda, and me, and has been a time for us to enjoy family and friends.

Our first Georgia Christmas was in 1987. As a family, we experienced surroundings that were quite different from previous years. But as Lynne and Amanda unpacked the boxes of ornaments and other Christmas decorations and began to place them in our new home, the old familiar spirit of the season seemed to settle into our hearts and spread throughout the unfamiliar rooms.

The handmade needlepoint stockings were hung carefully, and the napkin holders made by my mother and Amanda were set out for family meals. Each different ornament placed on our Christmas tree reminded us of a past holiday, different because it was celebrated in another city or home, but the same in terms of its special meaning for each of us.

Sam & Colleen Nunn

Christmas is a time when we come together to celebrate the birth of Jesus Christ and the spirit of peace, and it is also a time of special closeness as a family.

After the 1972 Senate election, our family had to settle in Washington in the middle of the Christmas holidays. It was a memorable occasion for many reasons, but extremely hectic. Yet in the midst of uprooting our family from so many of its traditions, a new family tradition was born that Christmas.

Since we moved so quickly, all of our Christmas ornaments were still at our home in Perry. We decided then to make our Christmas ornaments by hand instead of buying new decorations.

Our children were ages three and six when they began creating their own decorations, and this continued through grade school. They painted plastic Santa Clauses and angels and put them in a hot oven to shrink. They decorated sea shells, sand dollars, pine cones and the hulls from pecans and walnuts. They wove yarn around popsicle sticks; made cut-outs from felt and construction paper; stuffed cut-out calico candy canes and Christmas trees with cotton batting; made shadow boxes out of egg shells; and constructed bird feeders from plastic pill cylinders and cardboard.

They learned that you can make any Christmas special with a little creativity and perhaps a little less commercialism. Each year we now enjoy a tree adorned with precious memories for all of us.

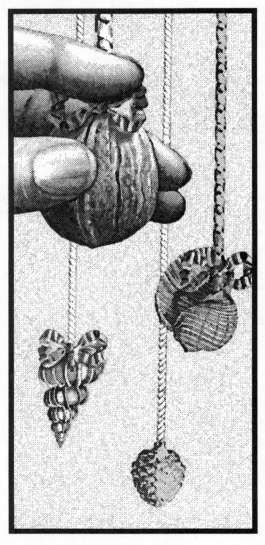

ILLUSTRATION BY MARTIN BOZONE

Christmas Traditions

John & Sue Wieland

Christmas is tradition! One of our favorite traditions as we celebrate the true joy of Christmas is the reading of *Let's Keep Christmas*, a sermon by Peter Marshall who was a Presbyterian minister from Scotland known for his powerful prayers.

First, though, comes our traditional Christmas supper—an unusual but tasty, filling, and easy-to-prepare meal of oyster stew, waldorf salad and peppermint ice cream. Then, there's the last-minute wrapping of surprises to be put under the tree. Finally we, listeners and readers, old and young, gather in a circle in the living room to share this wonderful book.

Our family has read this sermon together every Christmas, faithfully, for many years, with only the readers changing. Each year the glorious message of the real meaning of Christmas is ever fresh, ever powerful, ever special. Each year we are lifted up by Peter Marshall's words, which remind us that Christmas isn't in the stores but in our hearts—and that we must remain open to the spirit of Christmas each and every day of the year, not just on Christmas day.

Every year we are comforted and inspired anew by Peter Marshall's powerful reminder of what Christmas really is: God's promise, and our hope.

Dan Graveline

A conundrum is a riddle, where the answer is a clue to other questions, which lead to an answer. If that sounds like fun at Christmas time, you're right!

In my family, we each wrap a special gift and write a riddle about the package. Then, everyone guesses at the clues. The winner gets to open the gift, and to figure out what it means. My mother started this tradition as a way of making Christmas fun and exciting when there wasn't much money to spend on Christmas gifts.

One Christmas my wife and I wrapped a package of pink diapers, and wrote a riddle about the package.

Maybe our riddle was too specific. Or maybe it was just the happiness which radiated from our faces. In any event, the riddle was quickly solved: we were expecting a little girl!

That was a special Christmas for us, knowing that a little daughter would soon brighten our lives. And the conundrum was a fun way to share our pleasure with our loved ones. It just goes to show that special Christmases don't come from big, expensive presents. They come from sharing meaningful events and simple traditions with your family.

Larry Munson

As a young boy in Minneapolis, I could count on Christmas being the same every year. It never varied.

The snow was always there. It started snowing around Thanksgiving, and from then on we didn't see the ground for months.

On Christmas Eve, my parents, my sister, and I loaded the presents in the car. And off we went to spend the evening with my grandparents, my aunt and uncle, and their one child.

As we stack the presents around the tree, we grow more anxious by the minute. My sister, my cousin and I are eager to dig into that pile of presents.

But first we must sit down and eat a huge turkey dinner!

And now that dinner is over, all the grown-ups gather in the kitchen to do the dishes. Another forty minutes. Meanwhile us kids are going bonkers thinking about what's in those boxes.

Finally we open the presents. Now I'm ready to go off and play with my new toys.

But wait! Another ritual. First we gather around the piano to sing Christmas carols. Patience, Larry, patience.

Now, many years later, I realize how neat that really was. 'Cause hardly anybody gathers around the piano to sing Christmas carols anymore.

We never varied from the pattern.

Then on Christmas Day we went to St. Paul to another aunt and uncle's house. Lots of cousins here. Another big Christmas dinner.

My uncle owned a meat market. So we always had something special. One year a goose. Another year a stuffed pig. And I'll never forget the forty pound northern pike with the apple in its mouth. Forty-four inches long.

Isn't it amazing what you can dig out of your memory when you really try?

ILLUSTRATION BY LYN ALBERS

Kore Thompson

When you were three or four years old, was your Christmas anything like mine?

On Christmas Eve my family got together with my little friend Janie's family. It was at our house or hers, depending on the year.

First we had our traditional dinner. It was probably a little different from yours—stuffed flounder, with bacon and lemon on top. Plus whatever food was the latest fad. One year, we had artichokes!

After dinner we exchanged presents between the families. And then we began to anticipate the arrival of Santa Claus. Talk about excitement—Janie and I were ready to jump out of our skin!

The most magical time of the whole evening was when our fathers gathered around the radio and fiddled with the knobs, searching for a report of the first sighting of Santa Claus. We listened with great interest as the announcer reported on Santa's progress, and what he was carrying in his sleigh.

Then our families departed with great haste. We had to get home before Santa arrived. We had to get out his milk and cookies. And the most difficult of all—we had to get to sleep in a hurry or he wouldn't stop at our house!

Dillard Munford

Christmas was a great time at my home in Cartersville, Georgia, and my stepmother, who in effect raised me after my mother was killed when I was three months old, taught kindergarten for about forty years and knew every trick there was to working with children.

One of her ploys was to have our house-man run around the house Christmas Eve night ringing a bell and then open a window into our living room, which was next door to the dining room where we were having dinner. The word was that if we ever saw Santa Claus we would not get any presents, so this became such a crucial issue that my older brother used to hide under the dining room table when he heard the bells ringing, so he wouldn't see Santa Claus.

An expansion of the Christmas spirit at our house was the use of "elfmen," who were Santa's helpers and who would visit the children when they got sick. This became such a wonderful program that we almost looked forward to getting sick so that we could be visited by the elfmen, who would leave notes on the bedside table and would leave little teeny tracks in the ashes as they came down the chimney. We children would, of course, write letters to the elfmen during the day and have them picked up and then get a response that night for the next day. Occasionally the elfmen would leave a little present, and we would leave pieces of candy and cake for the elfmen to eat during their visit. The elfmen program was expanded to elfmen playing tricks on our dogs and cats while leaving ashes on their heads or tying ribbons on the kittens, and it all made going to bed at night and awakening in the morning wonderfully exciting at that period in our young lives when we went through all the childhood diseases of measles, chickenpox, whooping cough, flu, and an occasional operation such as a tonsillectomy.

It's amazing what parents can do for their children to overcome various stages of hardships by just getting down to the children's level, and my stepmother was an expert at this.

It was rumored in Cartersville that Mrs. Marilu's private kindergarten was in such demand for the education, artistic and religious training she gave the young children, that children were enrolled at conception.

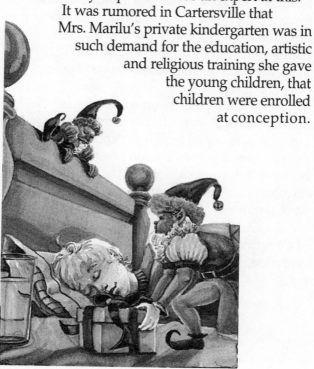

Deen Day Smith

Great-grandmother and Grandmother had feather mattresses on the beds in their homes. During the holidays, it was a joy to visit and be tucked into a bed in a cool room with only a few embers remaining from a fire in the fireplace.

Knowing that the softness of the down feathers and the sinking thrill associated with them would lure the children to play on the bed during the day, the ladies devised a creative plan which worked well. The grandmothers put treats between the mattresses for good little boys and girls.

During the Christmas season when the house was filled with Christmas spirit, each grandchild knew all kinds of homemade surprises awaited the small hands that reached between the mattresses. When the temptation to jump into the feather mattresses occurred, we were reminded of the forthcoming surprises.

Our family understood the true meaning of Christmas. We gave thanks for Christ and for everything we were given at our grandmothers' house.

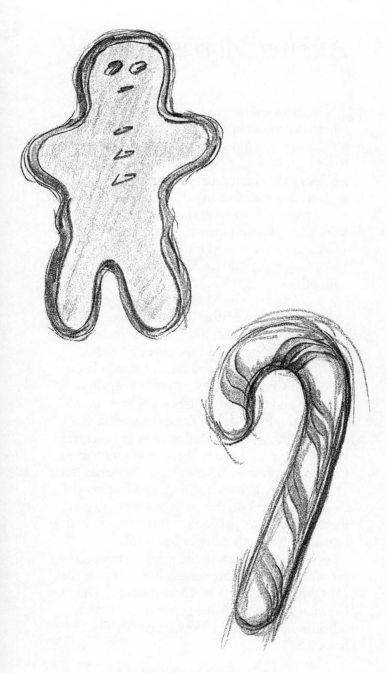

Aubrey Morris

As a kid on our farm in Roswell, I remember my father hitching the mules to the wagon so we could go into the woods to select a cedar tree. With our beautiful tree on the wagon we drove to Lebanon Baptist Church, where the tree was installed and trimmed with home-made paper decorations and red berries from the holly trees. Brown paper bags containing apples and candy were placed under the tree. Oh, the joy of looking at the tree in church and sharing it with others.

As a reporter at WSB I remember the very first lighting of the Christmas tree at Rich's. And every year after that I attended regularly, and promoted the event on radio.

As a husband and father I remember a particular Christmas about twenty years ago. My wife and three daughters and I were up at 3 A.M. because I was due at the radio station at 5 A.M. As I drove down Piedmont near Peachtree I was sad because I had to leave my family on Christmas morning. There was a Christmas tree lot with many trees remaining. The first rays of the sun reflected on the frosty branches to give the appearance of millions of stars shining in the branches. It was dazzlingly beautiful!

As I think about the role that trees have played in my Christmas memories, I realize that my favorite song is "Oh, Tannenbaum." The German title reminds me of the tree-covered hillsides in Germany. "How lovely are thy branches!"

Frank C. Jones

My mother and two of her sisters married Macon men. Beginning in the early 1920s, shortly after the first grandchild was born, the three sisters and their families would have supper together at someone's home during the Christmas season. This custom has continued for almost seventy years.

I recall vividly many of these family gatherings: singing Christmas carols; giving and receiving presents; eating delicious meals; seeing those who were home for the holidays; but, most of all, the warmth and love exhibited among the family members. Those who married into the family—"outlaws"—were at first overwhelmed by the event but over time have become among the most ardent advocates to continue the practice notwithstanding the increasing logistical problems. (More than sixty will attend in 1991.) We now have "family stationery" in a professional format listing the date of birth of each living descendant, and the dates of birth and death of deceased members.

This type of occasion may not appeal to some, and it may be impractical for others, but the idea that underlies it should be of universal application. A family can benefit at Christmas from any custom that helps to bond the family members together, that reaffirms the love and affection among the members of the family and that helps remind all of us of the blessings we receive from God throughout the year and particularly through the central event that we celebrate at Christmas.

A.W. Dahlberg III

For more than twenty years, my family, as well as my brother and sisters and their families, have been gathering for Christmas Eve dinner at our parents' Stone Mountain home.

The highlight of the evening always occurred just before everyone went home. When the grandchildren weren't looking, my father would sneak outside, climb a ladder to the roof, and call, "Ho, ho, ho, merry Christmas" down the chimney. When the kids were little, they'd look up the fireplace, trying to see Santa Claus. And then they'd tell their parents that they'd better hurry home, because Santa was on his way.

When the grandchildren were grown, they still loved this tradition. In fact, the oldest grandchild always made a point of saying to her grandfather, "Isn't it about time for the ho, ho, ho bit?" And even when our kids were in college and we were living in Birmingham, we'd make a special trip to Atlanta just to spend Christmas Eve with my parents—and to hear Santa's greetings of the season.

ILLUSTRATION BY LINDA MITCHELL

Zell Miller

The Miller home in Young Harris is the bedrock of our family. In the summer of 1932, shortly after my father died, my mother began to build a home for her and her two children—one so sturdy and enduring that it would last forever. She got the material for the house in 1932 with rocks from a nearby creek, designed the house herself, and with the help of some local workmen, built our home. We've spent every Christmas there ever since.

There were some times when I thought I wouldn't make it back. When I was eleven years old, my mother had moved us to Atlanta so she could work in the Bell bomber plant during the war. She didn't get off work on Christmas Eve until late in the afternoon, but we caught a bus and came on up to Young Harris, getting in at eleven o'clock that night. It was just as cold as could be; we went straight to bed.

The next morning, I got up, and she had built a fire. My aunt had put up a Christmas tree. I didn't get any toys or clothes that Christmas, but I remember getting a twenty-five dollar U.S. Savings Bond. And I felt mighty rich.

I remember another Christmas about ten years later. I was in the Marine Corps, and I had been on guard duty on Christmas Eve. When I got off guard duty, I caught a bus to come home, and I remember being on that bus when midnight struck on Christmas Eve. I got into Atlanta at two in the morning and went on to Macon to my sister's home, where my mother was staying.

My mother and I then borrowed a car, drove up to Young Harris and had a wonderful Christmas lunch and talked about old times. After lunch, I put on my splendid dress-blue Marine Corps uniform and went over to Andrews, North Carolina, to try to impress a certain young lady by the name of Shirley.

ILLUSTRATION BY BETSY KOOLS

Barbara Dooley

Football and bowl games always demand a lot of our time and attention during the Christmas season. So Vince and I try to keep Christmas in focus for our family by placing high priority on traditional family activities.

A lively time is had by all when the Dooley family gets together to decorate and create a Christmas tree of unique beauty. There is a background of lovely Christmas music. There are copious amounts of hot chocolate. And the inevitable heated debate about the location of lights!

And it's fun to create our traditional candy wreath. We begin with styrofoam covered with red ribbon. Then we pin 500 pieces of hard candy to the wreath. When this hangs in our kitchen it attracts our children and their friends and says "Welcome" to all.

And speaking of candy, may we share with you an old South Georgia recipe given to me by a south Alabama lady. It uses orange gumdrops and makes the perfect Christmas cake!

Orange Slice Cake

1/2 cup (2 sticks) butter
2 cups sugar
4 eggs at room temperature
3 1/2 cups all-purpose flour
1 tsp. ea. salt and soda
1/2 cup buttermilk
2 cups pecans, chopped small
16 oz. chopped dates
16 oz. orange jelly slices
1 tsp. ea. vanilla and lemon juice

Cream butter and sugar. Add eggs, one at a time, mixing well after each. Using 1 cup flour, toss chopped fruits and candy.

Dissolve soda and salt in milk and add to sugar/ egg mixture, alternately with flour.

Pour floured fruit mixture in and mix well. Bake at 250 degrees for 2 1/2 hours or until pick comes out clean. Makes one tube or 2 loaves. (If sitting for a week or so, add a jigger of bourbon a couple of times.) Cake freezes well.

Rosalynn Carter

There are a few Christmas traditions that our family enjoys: being at home together in Plains; trekking through our woods to find a Christmas tree that is just right and all joining in to decorate it; and of course, the usual good foods, which must always include the Plains Special Cheese Ring:

1 pound grated sharp cheddar cheese
1 cup mayonnaise
1 cup chopped nuts
1 small onion, grated
Black pepper to taste
Dash of cayenne

Mix; mold with hands into desired shape (I mold into a ring); place in refrigerator until chilled. To serve, fill center with strawberry preserves.

One of the nice features of working with Habitat is providing homes for others, so they can develop their own traditions.

ILLUSTRATION BY JILL DUBIN

Billy Payne

We would like to share with you a family tradition—our favorite Christmas dinner. . . Quail in Gravy:

In an iron skillet, melt 1/2 cup real butter. No substitutes.
Add 4 Tbs. flour and brown well.
Add 2 cups hot tap water and stir mixture until smooth.
Add to mixture:
2 Tbs. Worcestershire sauce.
2 Tbs. lemon juice
Stir.
Add cleaned, washed quail which has been salted and peppered to taste.
Cover and cook until tender in 325 degree oven, about two hours, basting often.
Serve with rice or grits.

If thicker gravy is desired, remove quail from sauce, and thicken gravy with flour. Return quail to sauce for serving.

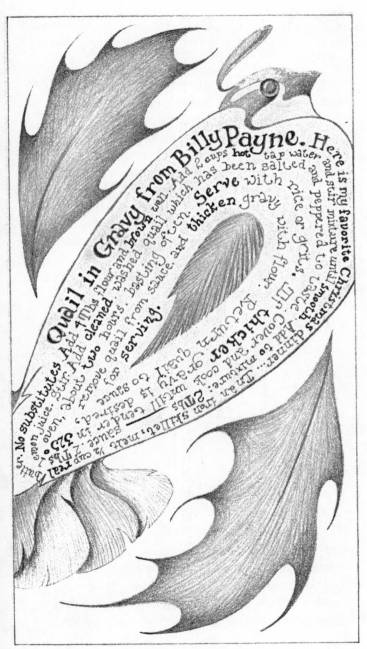

Quail in Gravy from Billy Payne.

Here is my favorite Christmas dinner ... Chicken quail tender in destined. In an iron skillet melt ½ cup real Butter. No substitutes. Add 4 Tbs flour and brown well. Add 2 cups hot tap water and stir mixture until smooth and peppered to taste. Add lemon juice. Stir. Add cleaned, washed quail which has been salted and peppered to taste. Cover and cook until ½ tender, in 325° oven, about two hours, basting often. Return quail to sauce: 2 Tbs. Serve with rice or grits. Cover and cook gravy ½ destined, in 325° oven. Remove quail from sauce and thicken gravy with flour for serving.

ILLUSTRATION BY KAREN STRELECHI

93

Betty Talmadge

Food plays a special part in the holiday festivities at Lovejoy. There is no better way to bring family and friends together than over a table that is covered with turkey, ham, and an array of sweets that'll have me signing up for the diet farm before New Year's

We even decorate with food. This tradition really started with Louise Hastings. . . a very talented floral designer and friend who decorated this house for parties and special occasions for years.

At Christmas, she designed a centerpiece around a Williamsburg apple tree.

The apples were secured on a wooden cone-shaped form. Louise's apple tree was even prettier than the ones in Williamsburg, because she went to great effort to find a variety of sizes of apples. She used large ones around the base of the tree and graduated to smaller ones

ILLUSTRATION BY LEROY SCOTT

on each row going up. She crowned the tree with a small pineapple and filled in around the apples with boxwood. . . . Sometimes the food I serve during the holidays provides an added decoration. I do a raw broccoli appetizer arranged in the shape of a wreath. I cut the top off a red bell pepper and fill it with dip for the center of the wreath. The top of the pepper can be sliced into pieces and arranged as a bow at the bottom of the wreath. A parsley wreath filled with cherry tomatoes is another edible decoration Louise devised. . . .

Another fun food decoration is the pig tree. We blow extra-large eggs and decorate them to look like little pigs with angel wings. Pieces of pipe cleaners are coiled and stuck in one end to make a tail, and a button is glued on the other end for a nose. Construction paper is cut in the shapes of ears and wings. For legs, take about a quarter inch by two-inch strip of paper and roll tight and glue to the bottom of the egg shell. Glue a small yarn bow on top to hang them by.

These fun decorations make dining during the holidays all the more exciting.

Nathalie Dupree

Christmas for me is a time of camellias
and occasional bouts of walking weather, mixed
in with days of rain that drop the temperature
and chill to the bone. I alternate between cover-
ing my pansies and camellia bushes with sheets
and old tablecloths at night to protect them from
the threat of a freeze to sitting in the sun like
a lazy cat, albeit with a jacket and gloves on. I've
been known to put the convertible top down
and the car heater on while delivering Christmas
goodies. And for the one in fifteen years when
it snows anywhere near Christmas, it is not
unusual to see pansies poking their heads up
through the snow, and when the snow melts
the next day saucily raising their heads to the
sound of snow rushing slickly off the magnolia
leaves as if it couldn't go fast enough to rid
the world of its inconvenience.

Where the turkey reigns supreme at
Thanksgiving, Christmas is the time of the ham.
Perhaps a goose, or quail, but most assuredly
a ham. Country ham is most traditional, but
unless there is one lurking in the closet (as an
increasingly daunting obstacle to the novice
cook), the tendency more and more is to use a
prepared one. Great care has to be exercised
to remove enough salt from the country ham to
please the palates of those who no longer use
much salt.

Christmas Eve is a time for glamorous
parties and for special moments. My friends
Amanda and George Olmstead (whose daughter

is my god-child) always have a buffet on Christmas Eve, after the early church service and before the late. It is a dress-up time, a time when all should be right in the world. We put aside our cares, and luxuriate.

A misty mean rain may make it impossible to find the curb for parking, but that doesn't daunt any of us. The house is always full when I arrive. There are dozens of children at all levels, the most dangerous being knee level, chasing each other as likely as not, although the velvet garments (perhaps bought a little big so they can be worn for several years) slow down the worst of them.

The grown-ups sip various potions, from iced tea to egg nog or bourbon and branch water. Coke is ever present, with Diet Coke wooing the teen-age girls, who eye the boys across the room.

We fill our plates with ham and fixings and catch up with people we haven't seen since last year, but meant to. There is always a cousin or two in the crowd, and it is a time to exchange information about births, deaths and divorces. When we feel warm and cozy enough it is time to go home to the world of ribbons and paper and undone duties to make the morrow the best it can be.

Special
Christmas
Memories

James L. Webb

There are mem'ries dancin' 'round
in my head of long ago
'bout my home near Fulton Bag Mill
and a family I loved so,
and of a long-haired boy a-scampering
to the nearby grocery store
to work to earn a nickel
'cause we were so very poor.
I can see the Christmas stockings, five of
them, all in a row,
near the scrawny Christmas pine
bedecked with popcorn and bows.
Not much was found under the tree
but in the stockings, some fruit (with luck),
and dinner wasn't ham or turkey or such
but a hen that I helped pluck.
Yet our Christmases were special,
precious memories so sublime
as jewels in the heart of a wild-eyed child
and a head now gray from time.

H. Dean Propst

A child's mind is capable of harboring the greatest of concerns. I still remember one such concern in my mind over fifty years ago.

Knowing that Santa Claus was a weighty individual, I became increasingly concerned one Christmas about his welfare during the annual visit. Our house had a very narrow chimney. I knew absolutely that, if he became stuck, he would never be unstuck.

My concern about his personal welfare kept me awake well into the evening on Christmas Eve. I was so worried that my house would be responsible for "killing Christmas."

Upon awakening on Christmas Day, I rushed into the living room, disregarding the gifts under the tree. Sticking my head into the (fireless) fireplace, I looked upward to the light. Seeing no obstruction, I knew then that Santa had safely come and gone and that whatever ill might have befallen him on that Christmas Eve, the Propst house was not to blame.

David R. Jones

On Christmas Day in 1985, the temperature dropped to fifteen degrees, and strong cold wind made it nearly unbearable to be outside. That evening I joined a small group of gas company employees and their families who braved the cold to celebrate the 130th anniversary of the lighting of Atlanta's first gas street lights.

We gathered at the Five Points MARTA station, where one of the original fifty gas lights was standing. (That light, the Eternal Flame of the Confederacy, has since been moved to Underground Atlanta.)

Television cameras rolled as one of our employees, dressed in a lamplighter's costume, climbed a ladder to reenact the lighting of the first lamp. The wind was blowing so hard it blew the flame out several times, but we soon prevailed. The program called for me to make some brief remarks. Then our whole group was to sing a Christmas carol. As I was speaking, I realized that the television crews weren't interested in what I had to say. More than any other part of the short program, the group singing was what they wanted to videotape.

The plan was for one of our employees, who sings very nicely, to lead the group in a rendition of "We Wish You a Merry Christmas." She would sing the verses, and we would all join in the chorus. As the cameras rolled, most of us had trouble making our lips move in the frigid weather. But I joined in the singing despite the fact that I can't carry a tune in a bucket.

I didn't realize that while I was singing the cameras were taking close-ups of several of us. That night, when I got home, I told my kids that the ceremony would be on the eleven o'clock news, but that I was too tired to stay up for it. Well, they watched it with some of their friends, and the next morning my wife told me that when the camera zoomed in on me—as I was singing off-key—the kids rolled on the floor laughing.

That Christmas Day will always be a source of pride for me as an important moment for Atlanta Gas Light Company. It will also be a source of some embarrassment—when the entire metropolitan Atlanta community had a chance to hear my own "special" rendition of "We Wish You a Merry Christmas."

Terry Kay

At Christmas, I like the smell of apples.

That is what we were given every Christmas at Vanna Junior High School, during a special assembly of grades one through nine.

Apples wrapped in paper. Large. Red. Sweet. The odor growing thicker with the unwrapping. The sound of bite and crunch from someone bold enough, or hungry enough, to start eating before the hand-outs were completed.

Apples and oranges and raisins on the stem.

Candy sticks.

For the boys, a pocket comb.

For the girls, hair pins.

Little gifts that seemed too fine to own.

And then Santa Claus would bolt in, yo-ho-hoing in a loud, familiar voice, and the older children would giggle with guesses about the pillow-fat man under the cotton beard while the younger children would stare at him in gleeful awe.

I cannot think of Christmas and not remember those years, those special December days of celebration, and the fly-back of memory is both joyful and melancholy.

On those days—more than any other time—I began to learn the difference between the haves and the have-nots.

The gifts we received were the same, and the yo-ho-hoing, pillow-fat Santa Claus treated us all with kindness and equity, but we knew—all of us knew—that it was only a temporary thing: the haves would have more, and the have-nots would not.

And the have-nots handled it better than the haves.

The have-nots hugged their gifts protectively and cherished them. The haves knew something better was waiting.

The have-nots took their apples home, to show.

The haves ate noisily on their way back to classrooms.

And that is the clearest vision I have of Christmas. Apples and children. Haves and have-nots.

But I think it's okay. I think that's what the day was about when it all got started.

Jim Peck

Two weeks before Christmas 1940, they brought my Dad home. I believe he was embarrassed. An Indiana coal miner since the age of twelve, he'd always been strong, and he'd always made a living with his hands. Now our family of six was dependent upon my older brother's job setting pins at the bowling alley.

My Dad was embarrassed, but we were glad to have him home from the Martinsville Sanitorium. Mom made pancakes his first morning back. When she heated the syrup, the tin exploded, scorching her arms and face with the hot liquid. During Mom's recovery, my Dad gained enough strength to take a WPA job sitting on a curb. Knocking mortar off of bricks. For no apparent reason.

It all sounds pretty melodramatic, to be sure, but then life is melodramatic. Comedy and tragedy are works of art.

But, we had an abundant Christmas that year. I was only six, so I didn't know why. Later, I was told. The local committee of the Democratic party there in Brazil, Indiana, brought us food and clothing and drums and dolls and puzzles and perfume and cigarettes—just as the WPA brought my Dad a measure of dignity. Not the church, not the government, not the United Mine Workers, not the coal operators. Christmas came from the marred and clumsy political party of FDR and the New Deal.

I know. I know. And I'm a cynic, too. And candidates of that brash party are looking a bit puny these days. Nevertheless, I cannot hear, nearing sixty, "Happy Days Are Here Again" as anything other than a holy Yuletide carol.

Gudmund Vigtel

Christmas Day in 1942 is a day I won't forget. I was seventeen then, living in my native Norway, which was occupied by the Germans.

My parents had been involved in clandestine resistance work and were obliged to flee for their safety to neighboring neutral Sweden. I had quit school to work on a farm, where I could get decent food. With my family gone, I decided to go to Sweden, too. I and a friend picked Christmas Day as a time when we figured that the German soldiers would be carousing and less vigilant.

We went by bus and on foot until we were near the snow-covered border. A local farmer, a stalwart man, risked his neck showing us how to stay clear of the Germans and cross the barbed wire they had laid along the Swedish border. It was easy going through the spruce forest until we hit that barbed wire. I got stuck there and before I could tear loose I learned something about panic. We got through and to safety eventually. That's when we said "Merry Christmas" to each other.

I joined the Free Norwegian Air Force in England and after the war came back to Norway, where I found my family safe and sound.

FINDLEY '92

ILLUSTRATION BY JOHN FINDLEY

Olga Goizueta

In Cuba, where we were born and grew up, we were especially blessed as children and then as young adults, since we celebrated two holidays.

It was customary to have a large dinner and family gathering on Christmas Eve, ending the evening with our attendance at Midnight Mass.

Then, on the sixth of January, we celebrated, as in all Latin countries, the arrival of the Three Kings.

Following that tradition, children received gifts, much as the child Jesus did hundreds of years ago.

Those memories of love, peace and good will have since remained with us.

ILLUSTRATION BY SYLVIA VEGA

Robert Shaw

On a cold Christmas Eve in the 1950s, having just completed a midnight broadcast with the NBC Symphony under Guido Cantelli, the Robert Shaw Chorale of thirty professional singers hurried by private automobiles to Riverdale just above Manhattan Island, where—by previous arrangement with Arturo Toscanini's son Walter they were to serenade the "Maestro" with their most recent recordings of carols.

Met at the door by Walter, who cautioned silence, we were surprised to be asked into the "grand salon." Arranging ourselves on the most impressive of marble staircases, we began to sing . . . and sang and sang.

The "Maestro" shuffled out from the adjacent library (where he had been watching wrestling on TV), tears rolling down his cheeks, insisting on more and more singing.

As we finished, doors were opened to a dining room table loaded with Italian pastries, cheeses and wines.

To each member of the group he said a personal and extended thanks throughout a Christmas Eve which lasted nearly to the break of day.

113

Amanda Davis

One of my most memorable Christmas seasons was when I was in the second grade. My father was in the military and we were just transferred from Texas to Albuquerque.

It was there that I saw snow for the first time in my life. Wow! It was great.

My parents decided to walk me to the neighborhood drugstore. We took pictures of the snow. We threw snowballs. And at the drugstore we all had hot chocolate. What a treat!

However, on the way back home it was windy and much colder. I asked my parents to hurry and take me home. But they wanted to take more pictures.

I began to cry. "I'm going home," I said. And with that I turned quickly around and headed for my warm house, just as Daddy snapped a picture—of my BACK.

How can I ever forget my first snow? This picture makes it a fond memory.

ILLUSTRATION BY LYNN ALBERS

Carmen Deedy

Papi was the first to touch the snow.

It lay in a web-like triangle in a corner of the landing that led to our new home in Decatur, Georgia. With the typical impulsiveness that would become my bedfellow throughout life, I had rushed toward it. My mother had deftly collared me before I could make contact. "Carmencita! No!"

"Pero, Mami, . . ." I had begun, twisting under her experienced grip. (The grip of a Cuban mother is tenacious and one that, no matter how gentle, may take a lifetime to wrench free of.)

"Nena, espera." Wait, my father had said.

My little body stopped its futile struggle and the small shoulders relaxed. My sister's eyes widened and my mother's narrowed as we all watched my father reach out his olive hand and rest his fingertips on the white powder.

One by one we took turns, silently. It did not burn. We did not stick to it, as my mother had predicted--much like an ice cube sticks to an impatient tongue.

It was like white, cold cotton candy that melted on contact.

We stood, looking at each other, in what must have been a funny little circle. In ill-fitting coats and shoes. My mother, for the first time in her life, in a pair of shoes and handbag that did not match.

Once you have lost your home, and seen

your neighbors' sons disappear, and traveled days to buy black-market meat because your children are so hungry that you end up pounding the table and telling them to shut up until everyone is screaming and crying, well, shoes and purses and hats never, ever matter in the same way again. Life is distilled to the essentials: food, shelter, medicine.

Now, we were in America. The place where everyone had the right to the fulfillment of these most basic human needs.

Yet, how very different this place was from our own beloved Havana. The day was bitter and overcast, the people kind but reserved.

"Mr. Agra? Mrs. Agra? Would you like to see the apartment now?" It was Mrs. Leslie, the German landlady who would become our benefactress and friend.

Much like the snow, the Americans we had encountered were beautiful, but cold. Little did we know at the time that, like the snow, they too would melt on contact.

Monica Kaufman

Christmas means breaking the language and color barrier:

I was an English tutor in Louisville, Kentucky, for Polish Jews who had immigrated to the USA. They had a daughter, and every week I would try to teach all of them English. I knew I was getting through when, at Hanukkah, the little girl asked her parents for a doll.

I was surprised and honored when it was black, like me.

Christmas
Gifts

Johnnetta B. Cole

I grew up in a warm and wonderful family in Jacksonville, Florida. Except for being teased by my older sister, having my pigtails pulled by boys in school and having to dust all of those chairs and table legs and what seemed like an endless array of things in the dining room, I was a pretty happy kid.

Christmas seemed like the time when everything good about being a kid was rolled into one big super-happy day. There were more

sweets around than I could possibly eat, dreams for particular toys came true, lots of relatives and friends would stop by, and we could stay up way past our bedtime.

It must have been the Christmas when I was about eight years old because I don't remember my baby brother being in our world yet—a great event that would happen when I was nine years old. I wished and wished for a pair of roller skates. It was the thing to wish for that year! And in our neighborhood, all of the kids were planning to meet on Christmas and take off en masse on a roller skating excursion.

It all came true; there they were, the prettiest pair of roller skates you've ever seen.

ILLUSTRATION BY LELAND BURKE

Even the key to tighten them seemed special to me. All went as planned until I was firmly on my skates, my Dad let go of my hands and I was ready to take off. And take off I did, for a great big fall. That happened what seemed like a hundred times! How humiliating!

My sister got it right away, but whatever we were trying, she always seemed to get it faster than I did. And all of the kids in the neighborhood seemed to be skating perfectly. Had they gotten their skates before Christmas and secretly practiced?

But each time I fell, my Dad firmly but lovingly said, "Get up now, baby, and try again." Finally it worked, I got it, the rhythm was there, I could roller skate! I still remember the fabulous joy of that moment.

I guess that's what life is about; learning to get up and try again. It was an important lesson to learn on a warm and wonderful Christmas day in Jacksonville, Florida.

Ben Jones

The Christmas I Learned to Fly

Time is elusive, increasing its preciousness as we age, growing in the knowledge that we have less of it left today than yesterday. That's why when we are six years old the two weeks before Christmas seem like a year. Now that I'm fifty, the year before Christmas seems like two weeks.

There was no heat in the upstairs of our old house by the freight yard. In the worst of winter, Mama would fill old whiskey bottles with hot water and put them at the foot of the bed to warm our toes. Soon we'd be snug between the quilts and the featherbed, deep in December dreams.

It was 1947. I was still at that age when believing in St. Nicholas was an unchallengeable act of faith. On Christmas Eve, when I could finally no longer keep my eyes open, I surely heard sleigh bells in the winter wind.

At first light on Christmas morning, I was awakened by my brothers' drowsy voices. Without signal, the race downstairs commenced, which always ended in a virtual three-way tie. My father, as was his habit, had risen long before dawn and had built a fine fire. By the glow of kerosene lamps our Christmas treasure waited, and fine ones they were in 1947: erector sets, Gilbert chemistry kits, a Sammy Baugh football, Hardy Boys books, a wind-up Victrola.

But rising above the bounty was love at first sight, for there by the tree stood sturdy perfection. It was a blue and yellow J.C. Higgins bicycle, proof positive that Santa knew Mr. Sears and Mr. Roebuck. I approached it tentatively, as if it were a mirage. It was too small for my brothers, and besides, they already had bikes. It was real to the touch. And there was a simple note attached: "To Buster, from Santa Claus. Thanks for the milk."

All that was left now for my life to be complete was to learn how to ride this beauty. On the winding road that ran past our house, beside the freight yard and down the docks, my brother Bubba pushed and held me steady while I grappled with the handlebars. And then there was the moment when I said "don't let go" and I heard his voice far behind me saying, "You're on your own." That's how the Wright Brothers must have felt at Kitty Hawk when man first took wings. I've been moving ever since and for that I'm grateful to my brother Bubba, to Mr. J.C. Higgins, to St. Nicholas, and to my parents, who taught me to fly.

Franklin M. Garrett

Since I was born in 1906 I have experienced quite a few Christmas seasons and I am a little hard put to pick out one that I can look back on as "extra special." However, I might cite Christmas 1918 as being in that category.

That was the Christmas I was presented by my parents with a bicycle for long rides and not just around the block on the sidewalks. It was a Niagara with a Morrow Coaster brake, but completely guiltless of a lot of gadgets on the handlebars. Indeed, my two legs were the propelling force.

At that time we were living on 13th Street near Piedmont Park in what is now called "Midtown" but at that time and long afterwards was simply referred to as "the northside."

As of Christmas 1918, World War I had ended a little more than a month before. During the war in 1917 Atlanta became the site of a major cantonment. It was called Camp Gordon and was located just to the east of Chamblee in DeKalb County. It was about twelve miles from where we then lived. So, I decided, for my first long ride, to pedal out and see what Camp Gordon looked like. My route was Peachtree Road, upon which the pavement ended at the DeKalb County line, where Club Drive now runs off. Anyway, a good dirt road is not bad for bicycling and I made the round-trip and got to see what a World War I cantonment looked like. (The site, incidentally, is now occupied by the remnants of the Naval Air Station of World War II and a small airport.)

Bobby Cremins

When I was about eleven years old all I wanted for Christmas was a basketball. I specifically asked for it. My heart was set on it.

When all the presents had been opened, there was no basketball. I guess I wasn't really disappointed. But then I wasn't really satisfied either. It seemed like that was going to be it. No basketball. It's not the end of the world.

Then my parents went behind the sofa and came out with the most beautiful round ball you ever saw. There it was. My very own basketball. I'll never forget how much I appreciated that gift.

That was the beginning of a love affair that lasts until this very day.

Alex Hawkins

When I was nine years old, I was excited over the prospect of finally receiving my most coveted Christmas treasure. A
Red Ryder BB gun.

I had been warned, repeatedly, of the danger of such a weapon. You know, the proverbial, "you'll put your eye out." Still, it remained the number one request on my Christmas wish list.

My older brother, fourteen, already had one which I, of course, was not allowed to handle. For the past three years I had been denied one. This was my year. I deserved one.

I had not blamed Santa for these oversights, having been told by my older brother some years before that Santa Claus was a fraud. For proof he had led me to the dark corners of our parents' closet and shown me Santa's gifts well in advance of Christmas.

As the Christmas of 1946 drew closer I uncovered, in my parents' closet, a brand new Red Ryder BB gun. Along with it was enough ammunition to last me well into the spring.

Smug and cocksure, I went to bed early Christmas Eve, knowing that the gun was not for my younger brother, six years my junior.

When I awoke that morning I raced into the living room and there, beside the tree, was a maroon bicycle earmarked for me. A bicycle? There was something wrong here. Was there really a Santa Claus and had he made an honest mistake in addresses? I was confused.

Later that day I discovered that the BB gun, hidden in my parents' closet, was found under the Christmas tree next door.

My faith in Santa was restored two years later when Red Ryder finally appeared under the tree *in my house.*

Sanford J. Jones

In 1988, my son was nine years old and my daughters were seven and twelve years of age. Our family lived in the country on a farm. All three of the children were very desirous of a four-wheeler to make their Christmas complete, couched under the pretense that a four-wheeler would help them to do their chores in and about the farm.

Their mother was very dubious about any thoughts of a four-wheeler, which might expose her children to danger.

As Christmas approached, the pleas became more and more frequent from the children for the one thing that to them had become the most important thing in life. It was obvious that there was not going to be a four-wheeler on the Jones farm in the near future.

As everyone knows, a father's judgments are not as sound as those of a mother, as

ILLUSTRATION BY SHARON WRIGHT

the maternal instinct seems to be more protective and realistic in the needs and care of children. This father was determined to find a way to secure a four-wheeler for what now had developed into three disappointed children who were not looking forward to a very happy Christmas. Of course, this four-wheeler had to be obtained over the consent of their mother and without placing my marriage in jeopardy. I, of course, proceeded to solicit the help of Santa Claus.

As all of us know, Santa Claus knows best, even above the judgment of doting mothers. And likewise, Santa Claus can do no wrong. Everyone knows that Santa Claus always makes the right decision on what gifts are best for the children. Therefore, it became apparent that the only person who could solve this dilemma had to be Santa Claus.

Upon contacting him personally, I found that he was very much in agreement with me and he promptly delivered a four-wheeler to the Jones children on Christmas day. My wife, to this day, still doesn't believe that Santa Claus is the one who really brought the four-wheeler, but I believe that part of her refusal to believe grew out of the fact that her two daughters abandoned the dolls and playhouse she had bought as soon as they realized that Santa Claus had overruled her and placed a new four-wheeler outside the door.

Thank goodness that no one has been hurt, for my wife would sure be mad with Santa Claus!

Dr. Werner Rogers

When I was five years old my family moved from Georgia to California. The holiday traditions were very different in California— my friends and I often went to the beach on Christmas day!

But every Christmas morning, among the other presents, there was always a special gift from home. Each year my grandmother, who still lived in Brunswick, sent a homemade fruitcake to the Rogerses of California. Opening the tin and unwrapping the cloth cover, I was instantly enveloped in a wonderful and powerful aroma that always triggered memories of a much earlier Christmas in Georgia.

The memory of Christmas day in 1945 remains vivid today. That morning I found a new train set under the Christmas tree—but that was not what made this holiday so special. World War II had ended only a few months

ILLUSTRATION BY SHARON WRIGHT

earlier, and my father and two uncles had just come home from the service. They were all spending the holiday at the Rogers house—the first family reunion in years and the first ever for me. It is my happiest childhood Christmas memory—an almost perfect day.

The only regret: Several days passed before I got to play with my new train set. My uncles decided it was a terrific toy—for them. While I only watched, the two men played with the train constantly until their visit ended.

Anne Rivers Siddons

Christmas Country

When I was a small child, Christmas presents all seemed to be the same present, though, of course, they varied. From Santa Claus, a doll every year. One year she cried, another year she drank from a bottle and wet, one year she had "magic baby skin," one year she was an eternal bride-to-be, as frozen on the eve of her wedding as Keats' unravished bride of quietness. One year, when I was twelve, she was a truly exquisite Alice in Wonderland, a perfect, fragile, mini-woman. Later that day, goaded by God knows what mute rebellion, spoiled perversity, what rampaging new hormones, I shot her with a new Daisy air rifle. Dolls were gone from my Christmas Country after that, to be replaced by charm bracelets and pink angora sweaters and record albums, by the flimsy, useless, spangled Christmas things that I still love to receive.

There would be outfits. A nurse's outfit. A cowgirl outfit, complete with fringed vest, six-shooter and miniature western boots. An appalling WAC outfit, for we seemed perpetually at war in that holiday country. Somewhere in my parents' house, small, grave me sights along the six-shooter into the camera still; lumpy, unlovely me salutes an unknown commander-in-chief under the patent-leather bill of a hideous flat-topped cap.

For my mother, a huge jar of blindingly purple bath salts that stank for days when she opened it. I had had my eye on it at Vickers'

Five-and-Ten for half a year, and Mrs. Vickers had had to scrape the grime of unwantedness out of its mock cut-crystal when I purchased it.

My father would open the miniature hat box with the wonderful, perfect little hat in it, and a certificate that said he could receive the hat of his choice at an Atlanta hattery. Always, he said it was just exactly what he needed. Always, he bought the same hat.

B. Franklin Skinner

Because my family is my greatest gift and joy, I have tremendous empathy for those who have no home or family to call their own. Perhaps that is why a story I read many years ago has stuck in my mind, and always comes back to me at Christmas time. It may be legend, but it has to do with an incident that took place in Baltimore back in the early part of this century.

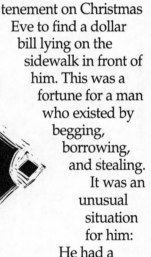

A tramp shuffled out of his skidrow tenement on Christmas Eve to find a dollar bill lying on the sidewalk in front of him. This was a fortune for a man who existed by begging, borrowing, and stealing. It was an unusual situation for him: He had a decision to make. What would he do with the money? It didn't take long—and he started off to buy drinks and to join the other tramps of the waterfront in their pathetic attempt to celebrate Christmas. But on the way, he passed a store, and his eye was drawn to a baseball bat in the

ILLUSTRATION BY SYLVIA VEGA

window. He stopped and stood staring, remembering how as a youngster who loved baseball he had longed for a real bat all his own. Then, impulsively, he decided to buy the bat and to take it to an orphanage nearby.

At the orphanage, he gave the bat to a homely, awkward little orphan boy who loved to play baseball, but who until that Christmas, like the tramp, had never owned a bat of his own. Years later, as an adult, that orphan would say it was the best Christmas gift he ever received. He was then known the world over as Babe Ruth.

It's part of the magic of Christmas.

Tommy Irvin

Although Christmas in the North Georgia mountains during my boyhood days was quite simple compared to today's extravagant celebration, it is that quiet, humble time I think of when recalling my most memorable Yuletide occasion.

Growing up on a farm in rural northeast Georgia, our Christmases revolved around our family and primarily included items we produced right there on the homeplace. Our Christmas tree, cut from the nearby woods, may not have had lights (we had just had electricity installed when I was a young boy, which consisted of a single light socket in each room), but the homemade decorations seemed to brighten our modest home.

We always looked forward to hanging our stockings on the mantel of our big fireplace, which, unlike the ornamental versions today, was our only source of heat. The fireplace was located in our big family room, which was originally a single-room, log-constructed house which had been added on to to accommodate a larger family.

My brothers and sisters and I were always excited to wake up on Christmas morning to find, inside our worn stockings, a baked sweet potato, a few seedling pecans from our farm and, if we were lucky, an orange. Oranges today could not possibly taste as good as that special piece of fruit we enjoyed on Christmas morning.

One Christmas particularly stands out in my memory. When I was about nine years old, I woke up on that Christmas morning to find not only a filled stocking but a shiny, brand-new red wagon. Although that wagon probably cost less than two dollars, it was my first "store-bought" toy. Most of our playthings were homemade. And while that sounds inexpensive compared to current toy prices, I know now how that purchase must have really strained our family's budget.

That little red wagon replaced the old wooden-wheeled wagon my father helped me make, which was often used to haul corn to the mill to be ground into cornmeal to feed our family. I pulled the new wagon with pride, and not only did I use it to help out with chores around the farm; I always enjoyed loading up my younger brother and pulling him down the dirt road that ran in front of our house.

The memories of that particular Christmas only serve to emphasize that it is not the quantity of presents and decorations which make the Yuletide celebration special. It is the fundamental gift of love from family and friends that provides the foundation of this holiday which we tend to forget was set aside to recognize the birth of the true Prince of Peace and Love. No matter how many earthly treasures and honors I might obtain, that little red wagon serves as a simple reminder of where I have come from, and that through His love, God is always watching over us.

The
Gift
of
Christmas

Eugenia Price

Christmas Alone Without Snow

In a very real way most of us are trapped by the trappings of Christmas, no matter how we try to remember the shining *reason* for the Holy Day. We're trapped by not wanting to cause hurt feelings, by not being able to face one or more family members forced to be alone on December 25, by reckless overspending, by exhaustion from malls and by long hours in the kitchen. But this is not going to be a suggestion for avoiding the entrapment, for "keeping Christ in Christmas." (How, in fact, does one keep Him out of it?) I am simply remembering one Christmas I spent *alone* under circumstances unusual enough so that no one was left out or hurt. My mother and father and only brother had gone to heaven, my best friend, Joyce Blackburn, with whom I share a home, was with her mother in Indiana and I hied myself to Savannah, where, during the writing of the Savannah Quartet of novels, I felt most at home.

Christmas Eve and Christmas Day alone? Yes. Except for the One whose birthday we are supposed to be celebrating! He *was there.* Of course, I missed my family. Of course, I missed Joyce, but my conscience was clear and that Christmas some years ago turned out to be one I'll never, never forget. No one had to tell me to "keep Christ in Christmas" or to lighten up on the commerciality. My quiet hotel room held no presents to open, none to mail or wonder about--all that had been handled before I hopped in my car on December 23 for what lives still in my memory as the most deeply meaningful Christmas of my entire life.

Christmas in the South sounds artificial to Northerners who, like me, grew up hoping for white Christmases. But Christmas on St. Simons Island, where I live, can be, thanks to the glorious way in which God does His own decorating in our remaining stands of woods, not only warm enough to stroll outside, but a spectacle of sheer beauty. (And I'm not speaking of the usual garish display of colored lights in which Southerners indulge, too.) He decorates His woods with the reddest branches of holly and cassina berries and, wonder of wonders, He even leaves behind scarlet creeper and tupelo leaves on a few deciduous trees. To me, though, most breathtaking of all, He drapes any willing tree and bush and scrub oak with golden-leaved bullis grapevines, so that almost every growing tree is a veritable holiday treat! (One recent Christmas on St. Simons Island delighted kids and amazed adults with a few inches of snow which actually stayed on the ground and on the branches of dark green live oaks and cedars for well over a day. Even the palmettos and palm trees held the now odd-looking white stuff and actually looked a bit silly.)

I used to love white Christmases in my youth. I loved that one here in coastal Georgia, but glistening snow (and it does stay clean here) and colored electric lights and expensively wrapped gifts do not a real Christmas make.

I feel I experienced the true authenticity of Christmas, the Holy Day on which God gave us His greatest gift, on that one Christmas in Savannah spent alone with Him, whose Birth we celebrate. I experienced the unforgettable hours *inside* a peace uninterrupted by a single jangle or a single duty gift or greeting card. Those were all piled in my kitchen when finally I reluctantly abandoned the light of my blessed solitude and drove home.

The Light was still inside me, though, and the peace.

Ruth A. Schmidt

My first Christmas in the South, if you count Florida as the South, was spent with my parents in that state in the 1950s. As one who was born in Minnesota and grew up where Christmas was almost always white and certainly cold, I found it very difficult to acquire a Christmas spirit among the greenery and the orange groves of Florida. I was absolutely scandalized by seeing Christmas lights strung on orange trees and found everything about this non-white, non-northern Christmas to be objectionable. However, probably growing tired of my complaints about a Christmas culturally determined, my father reminded me that what I was seeing in Florida was probably closer to the climate of the Holy Land than what I was used to in Minnesota. That gave me paus and stopped my complaints.

It seems to me that it was a wonderful lesson on how much the trappings of Christmas, the white Christmases,

 ILLUSTRATION BY SARAH KENNEDY

the family customs of exactly what *we* do at
Christmas, have come to color our whole per-
ception of the celebration of Christ's birth.
Mistaking the externals for the real meaning
is a common problem for all of us, and I
will always be grateful for my father's reminder,
which applies not only to Christmas (which I
dearly love to celebrate in any clime) but also to
the rest of life.

Michael Egan

The Christmases of 1950 and 1951 will always be remembered as being uniquely different.

In 1950 I was Duty Officer at the stockade at Fort Dix, New Jersey. It was Christmas Eve and I walked around doing bed checks until 6 A.M.

In 1951 I was on a hill somewhere in Korea. The priest said Mass off the hood of a Jeep.

In both cases I was a long way from home. And when I began to feel sorry for myself, I thought of all those who were less fortunate than I, and how lonely Mary and Joseph must have been that night in Bethlehem.

Being able to attend Mass on both of these occasions brought a true feeling of the religious holiday. None of the commercial trappings to distract from the real meaning of the day were present.

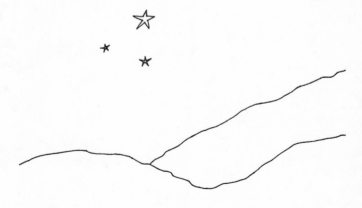

ILLUSTRATION BY ELIZABETH DAUGHERTY

Herman Talmadge

My father was in politics and the children in college. It was difficult for the family to get together except during Thanksgiving and Christmas, so these holidays were especially special to us.

Most people overlook the religious significance of Christmas. Christ arrived on earth to redeem mankind and enable us all who believe in Him to achieve everlasting life. It is a time when we should realize that we are on earth because of our Maker, and we should renew ourselves with the scriptures from the Bible.

Mack & Carolyn Mattingly

Over the years we have maintained a tradition of writing a Christmas poem that serves in place of a newsletter and that expresses our awe over the miracle that brings us together from wherever in the world we are and causes us to celebrate Christmas. These are concluding lines from a recent year's message:

Our granddaughter Hannah with twin -
kling brown eyes
And with laughter that banishes
sadness or sighs
Comes pattering in on the
fleetest of feet,
Or, chattering, brings in a
book for a treat,
And we all settle down to
read once more the reason
Our old world can take heart
in this singular season
Of loving and giving
because of God's gift
To a world that without
Him is lost and adrift.

ILLUSTRATION BY LINDA MITCHELL

Kenny & Carol Leon

Christmas is a special time for us, a time of joy with a hope for peace. The season reminds us of the possibilities that life holds and the wonder each new day brings. Our first Christmas was a realization of the need and desire to keep the spirit of Christmas in our hearts all year long.

That Christmas our home was filled with "the feel of Christmas"... a fresh-cut tree, the smell of holly, the carols, twinkling lights and friends—things we love and still do love to have around us. Then one night as we sat in a soft darkness enjoying the sparkle and twinkle of the lights we began to talk about the penetrating spirit of Christmas which cuts through the commercialism and greed. . . that spirit of Christmas continues to offer its gifts of life, love and celebration. We talked into the night, and thoughts fell from our mouths as the lights blinked and twinkled. We dwelled on the celebration of the Child and the gift that Child brought to the world.

With growing excitement we realized that the joy we felt in working with young people in the arts could be reflected upon during this season. Our commitment as well as our responsibility could be increased. Each Christmas would bring into focus the specialness each child brings to the world. Each Christmas would bring into focus the wonder and anticipation of life. Each Christmas would remind us that life is to be celebrated. Indeed, it is cause for celebration.

As the lights of Christmas twinkled and sparkled in our home, we vowed to capture some of that sparkle and keep a little with us throughout the year. Long after the tree is discarded and the lights are taken down, we can look at each other, when things look darkest, and we can remember the light and let it shine.

W. Frank Harrington

Some of my most vivid memories concern Christmas. I remember Christmas as a boy on a South Carolina farm. My mother would prepare for weeks. Fruitcakes would be baked. Nuts would be shelled—English walnuts, pecans, almonds, Brazil nuts. Fruit would be purchased and it was with a great sense of contentment that we would sit around the fire in the evening and watch my father peel an orange without breaking the peel. We watched for the long, long piece of orange peel. Today a fresh orange is a great treat for me, because when I was a boy we had oranges and tangerines only at Christmas.

Family would often come from far and near. They would stop by and share stories of their family. My mother would dispatch me on my bicycle to carry treats of great variety to our neighbors—fruitcakes, cookies, packaged nuts. And then, there was the anticipation of gifts that we would share. We exchanged Christmas lists in our family, and on that list were things we were hoping for, dreaming about.

In our own family, some of my most precious memories center on the word "sharing." With our daughters, Susi and Vicki, and Vicki's husband, Harold, and our grandchildren, Carolina and Michael, Sara and I eagerly share the holidays together. Of course we exchange gifts, but more than anything else, we share fellowship, stories of yesterday, hopes for tomorrow, and we enjoy each other. It is a special time of family sharing.

In our church Christmas is a time of sharing. We share our time with those who are carrying heavy burdens. We reach out in love not only to those who need us, but to each other in friendship. It all centers on the word "sharing." It is a time like no other for turning our thoughts outward. A time to share the beautiful story of Christ's birth. A time for celebration through our music, stories, times of fellowship together.

It is my hope that during this special time of year you will let the joy of God's gift surge through you soul. Fill your hearts with the promise He brings, and share that joy with your family, with your friends.

ILLUSTRATION BY RUTH MITCHELL

Ernest A. Fitzgerald

It was the day before Christmas. The mountains were covered with snow. The tiny frame church on the upper reaches of the Tuckasegee River was packed. The purpose was to hold the funeral for a father and husband who had been killed the day before in a logging accident. He left behind a widow and eight children, the oldest of whom was seventeen.

I had read the funeral service and offered what I hoped would be words of comfort to the bereaved family. Just before the benediction, a tall, handsome mountaineer stood and asked permission to say a word. He came down front and addressed the people present.

"Our friend and neighbor is gone now," he said. "He lost his life in the same dangerous work most of us do every day. The funeral has been nice, but this man's family needs some help. I want us to take a collection for this woman and her children."

Without another word he took his cap and began to move through the congregation. When all had had the opportunity to give, he took the money and placed it in the hands of that young widowed mother. His weather-beaten face became soft and kind. His usually cold blue eyes were misty. With a gentle voice he said to the woman, "If that ain't enough, you let me know."

It's been nearly a half-century since that funeral service on that cold Christmas Eve. Not before or since do I ever remember receiving a collection at a funeral. But through the years I have come to believe that this thoughtful mountaineer helped us to share in the most Christian funeral I have ever held. I am sure he captured the true meaning of Christmas when he reminded us that we who are followers of the man from Bethlehem must share our abundance with those who have so little.

ILLUSTRATION BY JOEY HANNAFORD

Christmas
Is
for
Giving

Lewis Grizzard

The Christmas I remember most, my father, an Army captain, had duty until noon on Christmas Eve. I waited for him at the screen door, sitting and staring until that blue Hudson—"The Blue Goose," as my father called it—pulled into the driveway. I ran out and jumped into his arms.

"Ready for Santa?" he asked.

"I've been ready since August," I shouted.

But before we could settle in for our Christmas, my father had to take care of a problem. He had found this family—the man out of work, in need of a shave and a haircut, and his wife crying because her babies were hungry. My father, whatever else he was, was a giving man. He couldn't stand to have when others didn't.

"They're flat on their butts and it's Christmas," I remember him saying to my mother. "Nobody deserves that."

So he somehow found a barber willing to leave home on Christmas Eve, and he took the old man in for a shave and a haircut. Then he bought the family groceries. Sacks and sacks of groceries. He bought toys for the kids.

We didn't leave them until dusk. The old

man and the woman thanked us, and the kids watched us with wondering eyes.

I slept with my parents that night and we cried ourselves to sleep. Next morning, I had my pistols and my hat and my picture of Hopalong Cassidy.

It was a Christmas a man can carry around for a lifetime. Each year at Christmas, with my father long since in his grave, I thank God that one is mine to remember.

Chuck Dowdle

As a native Atlantan, I feel that Christmas is just not Christmas unless it's spent in the sports capital of the South. Fortunately, all but a handful of my forty-two Christmases have been right here.

Naturally, there are all of the memories of the lighting of the Great Tree, visiting Santa Claus at any one of this town's great Santa hangouts, riding the Pink Pig at Rich's and taking part in my church's various Christmas events.

But the Christmas I will always remember is one that occurred not too long ago. Christmas 1985. My wife and I had just moved to Atlanta. For me, this was a return home from Miami, where I had worked for the previous dozen years. For my wife, it was her first southern Christmas. She's from Michigan.

I made certain that she understood what Christmas in the deep South was all about, and even nicely covered the fact that she'd probably have to slide by without snow! But despite that wintry shortcoming, I believe that she would agree with me, that Christmas of 1985 was the best we've ever had.

I came home from work one night to discover that my wife Clarice had come upon the name of a family in Jonesboro that was in need. The father was unemployed, the mother did not work, and there were three small children. Two boys, one girl—the girl a victim of Down's Syndrome.

Clarice decided that we would bypass our gifts that year, and instead she spent the money to buy toys, clothing, and food for that family. On Christmas Eve morning we delivered all of the presents my wife had carefully shopped for, and as we rounded the corner of this family's street, we noticed the three kids holding hands, standing in their yard awaiting the arrival of our gifts.

For the first time in my life, I was Santa Claus. In '85 we had no children. So for me, giving these gifts to these kids was a new experience. A great experience. An uplifting experience. A true Christmas experience.

Clarice and I now have a daughter. I love her dearly and I want her to always have wonderful Christmas holidays. I only hope that unlike her father, she won't wait till her mid-thirties to experience the true meaning of the holiday.

Millard & Linda Fuller

On Christmas Day in 1965 Linda and I were with the folks at Koinonia Farm in southwest Georgia. We were so impressed with their simple lifestyle and their utter devotion to Jesus. They had a program called "Bikes for Tykes," wherein they asked for donations to be used to purchase bicycles and tricycles for low-income youngsters who would otherwise not have anything for Christmas.

On this particular Christmas Day we rode through the countryside in a little truck, passing out the bicycles and tricycles to youngsters living in out-of-the-way places in one-room, unpainted shacks. Near the end of the day we gave our last bicycle to a little boy, and he was so excited about having it. But then his little sister appeared and began to cry because she was not going to get a bicycle. The boy looked at his bike, looked at us, and looked at his little sister. Then, he just quietly rolled it over to her and handed her the bicycle.

It was very touching to see that kind of sharing and giving on the part of a little boy who, with all of his heart, wanted a bicycle. But he was more concerned about sharing with his broken-hearted little sister than he was about having a bicycle himself.

The whole experience was tremendously exhilarating and brought us back to the real essence of the spirit of Christmas.

ILLUSTRATION BY SUZANNE ROYAL

Wyche Fowler, Jr.

Christmas has always been a special family time for me.

One of the Christmases that I remember well was the one we celebrated when I was about eight years old.

It was the Sunday before Christmas. As was our family's way, my mother, father, sister and I all went to church for Sunday school and service. This year we brought two orphans, a boy and a girl, the same ages as my sister and I, from the Baptist Children's Home to our house to spend the day with us.

My mother made her traditional Sunday dinner of fried chicken, rice and gravy and beans, followed by ice cream and her chocolate cake.

The boy, the girl, my sister and I then went out in our backyard to cut down a tree. Then the four of us spent the afternoon decorating our Christmas tree before we had to take the boy and girl back.

This Christmas made a lasting impression on me. It taught me the importance of sharing with those who are less fortunate.

Sam & Doris Massell

Our greatest recollection of the Christmas season has always been the warmth that's radiated between even the most distant of strangers. No matter what the station in life, one can't help but feel enriched by his fellow man's demeanor, which becomes its most gracious at this time of the year. We find ourselves smiling more, exchanging greetings and exuding generosity.

Before we had our own children, each year the two of us would buy several toys, wrap them at home and then drive through some of the lower-income areas and anonymously hand them out to little boys and girls we saw along the way. Now our son and two daughters are grown and do similar acts of charity, and don't even know we indoctrinated them—or did we?

There's no greater evidence that "it's better to give than to receive" than the gleam in a child's eyes in this scenario. Giving at every level, in fact, is a godsend, and those who do receive a rich reward in the very joy of the occasion.

Brenda Wood

When I was in high school, my mother and I decided to include a fellow student in our family at Christmas. He was very poor and needed clothing. So we took him shopping and bought him presents. He needed to know somebody cared. His smile and his friendship were our reward for giving thought and time to a needy person. We learned a valuable lesson in giving.

Later in my life, God gave my husband and me a very special gift, our first child, just four days after Christmas. And every year at Christmas we think of God's generosity in giving us His Son, Jesus, and our daughter, Kristen, at this time of the year.

Homer Rice

My most memorable Christmas is the one I spent in the Philippines during my tour of duty in the Navy during World War II. I was in charge of supplies and had much responsibility even though I was barely eighteen. This was also the first Christmas I had ever spent away from my family in Kentucky. Even though this should have beena very unhappy time because of being away from my family, it has become my most treasured Christmas memory.

The chaplain of our company, Chaplain Deer, who was from Texas, asked some of us to help make presents for the Filipino children. On Christmas Eve we delivered our gifts to a small church in Bataan and had the joy of watching these young children open their gifts. The gifts were handmade and by today's standards would be considered worthless. However, the war had left these young children with no pleasant memories of Christmas and in many cases, many Christmases with no gifts at all. They were over-whelmed. Their joy and excite-ment over the little gifts that we were able to make is something I will always remember. For them, Christmas had returned.

Today, our three beautiful daughters have given us seven wonderful grandchildren. Each year at Christmas, our grandchildren enact the Christmas story for our family. Seeing my own grandchildren's happy faces always re-minds me of the faces of the Filipino children on that Christmas so long ago. In their faces filled with joy and excitement is the true meaning of Christmas.

ILLUSTRATION BY SUZANNE ROYAL

John Pruitt

Christmas 1965 I was serving with the U.S. Army in Korea. I was a single man a long way from home with not much to look forward to in the way of Christmas cheer.

A family I knew in Avondale contacted me to ask a favor. Their son was a missionary in a remote leper colony on the southern Korean coast. Because they were concerned about sending their Christmas presents to the family through the Korean mail system, they wanted to send the presents to me through the military mail so I could personally take them to the family.

So, early one December morning I boarded a train for the village of Soonchun carrying a bag full of toys and other presents. Twenty-four hours later, after an exhausting ride, I was there.

I was welcomed with open arms by this family, especially the three little girls, who viewed me as a sort of Santa Claus because of the gifts I was bearing.

The next few days were wonderful, as I enjoyed Christmas far away from home with a grateful family that took me in and treated me as one of their own. Now that I have a family of my own, I often look back fondly on that Korean Christmas as one of the most memorable.

Jerry Glanville

It was Christmas Eve in 1989. I had coached my last game for the Oilers in Houston, Texas.

The Second Baptist Church in Houston asked me to conduct Christmas Eve services for some very special children. They were seriously ill. And they were brought to the church from Louisiana, Oklahoma and Texas.

This was a huge, round church. And it was filled with these children, each one holding a candle.

I have always believed in the power of unselfish prayer. And I truly believe some kids were helped during that candlelight service.

After the service, I met all the kids who came through the sanctuary. It was the most heartwarming experience I have ever had!

Joe Washington

A few years ago, I was invited, along with other media and sports people, to join in a unique Christmas program. Its purpose was to take underprivileged children shopping for Christmas.

The children were from shelters—some abused, some abandoned by their parents.

I'll never forget Marcus. He was about eight or nine years old. He was always smiling. Always bouncing around.

When I asked him what he wanted, he said he wanted clothes. Can you imagine an eight-year-old boy asking for clothes for Christmas?

So we went to some clothing stores. He picked out a jacket, a cap, some pants, a sweater, some socks. We had been given $75.00 to spend, but that only got us started.

Then we went to eat. We had a good time.

When we returned to his home, he invited me to come inside. He wanted me to meet his friends. And he wanted me to see his closet.

He opened his closet door. One pair of pants and two shirts. All of his worldly goods. He was so proud.

Marcus had a strong impact on me. He put it all in perspective. He was way ahead of me.

He was making do with what he had.

Benny Andrews

The Christmas of 1973

I had been directing a prison art program for several years through an arts organization I co-chaired, The Black Emergency Cultural Coalition. About an hour before my family and I were scheduled to sit down for our Christmas dinner, there was a knock on the front door.

I put down the part of the dinner I was helping to prepare and opened the door to a person who looked like a character out of *Oliver Twist*. Dressed in tattered clothing and clutching a half-filled laundry bag, this person, whom I shall call Bill, asked, "Are you Benny Andrews?"

"Yep, that's me," I replied, taken aback by his sad appearance.

"Well, I hate to burst in on you like this, but I just got in from being released from Greenhaven [prison], and I was told if I couldn't find anyone else in the world to help me, then I was to come and see you."

There was truth in that, as word had been passed along in the prison system about me, since I'd given a few dollars and some clothing, and even assisted ex-prisoners to get jobs. Nevertheless, these acts had taken place at my studio or in prisons, never at home, much less when I was about to sit down to something as special as a family Christmas dinner.

He just stood there for what seemed like eons, and my first impulse was to hand him a few dollars and bid him goodbye. Then, I thought about what Christmas could stand for, so I invited him in and, to make a long story

ILLUSTRATION BY BENNY ANDREWS

short, had him join the family for dinner. Afterwards, I gave him a Christmas gift of money and all of us wished him good luck and a happy New Year.

Two Christmases later, 1975, among my cards was one from Bill. It read,

"Chances are you've long forgotten me, because I know guys like me come through your life every day, but I just want to tell you how much it meant to me to have dinner with you and your family that Christmas day.

"You didn't give me a chance to tell you how desperate I really was on that day. I'd been mugged earlier and had only my bus ticket to go home to St. Louis. I'd decided that if you didn't help me I was going to mug somebody to get money for food. Of course, I could have been caught and gone right back to prison. Instead, I went on home and resumed my family life with my wife and two children. I have a good job now and feel very good about myself.

"So, thanks, and I'm trying to help others just like you helped me."

Bill really made our 1975 Christmas dinner much more than food, gifts, and revelry. It made us feel like we were part of something bigger and much more lasting: a network of sensitive and responsive human beings.

Maynard Jackson

As one of six children, my parents instilled in each of us, at a very tender age, the values of giving, sharing, and helping those less fortunate than we were.

Those values have profoundly influenced my life, first as an attorney and then as a public servant. In this my third term as mayor, I am confident that we are making a difference.

Times are tough now and the needs are much greater, but as a city we cannot rest until all of our citizens have adequate food, clothing and shelter. Though the holidays are often remembered from a child's perspective, it is the spirit of this occasion which endures.

The needs of Atlanta's poor and homeless have been well served by Habitat for Humanity and the many "helping hands" who provide hope and homes for our needy. As we celebrate the blessings of yet another year, let us join together as a family and continue to seed the holiday spirit.

ILLUSTRATION BY KAREN STRELECHI

177

A
Christmas
Housewarming

James P. Lyke

When I was a young boy growing up on the south side of Chicago at Christmastime, my older brothers and sisters would take me and my friends out of the projects to visit the exquisite Christmas displays of the manger, Christmas trees and lights, etc., in the very wealthy areas of Chicago's north side. At the time, I never gave any serious reflection to my temporary escape into a Christmas Disney World or had any insight into the way "they" lived and the way "we" lived. It was all about wonder and awe and excitement.

Now, seasoned with age and some learning, I see more and understand more why Habitat for Humanity has made a dwelling place for my childhood remembrances and helped me construct a new home in which to house my hopes and dreams. Habitat gives me a spiritually uplifting sense of wonder and awe and excitement. Habitat is truly "Christ among us."

ILLUSTRATION BY LEROY SCOTT

181

Larry Arney

During the Christmas season of 1989, many of the Christmas "traditions" that I had followed since locating in Atlanta eight years ago were changing. In fact, my life in 1989 had changed substantially.

In January of that year, I left architectural practice to become the Director of Habitat for Humanity in Atlanta. Throughout the year, I was adjusting to a new job with more than a few uncertainties and with little experience. The job was so unlike architectural practice. Could I do it? Would I be effective at promoting the organization? And would the public respond to Habitat on a continuing basis? Looking back on it, I think I was searching for a "sign" to tell me that I had done the right thing.

Our Homeowner's Association sponsored a Christmas party that year, the first one ever for us. The homeowners decided that they wanted to honor the construction staff at Habitat. After all, each of these houseleaders was directly responsible for leading groups of volunteers and homeowners in building their homes.

Although I am not a part of the construction staff (my job deals with the less glamorous administrative details), I was invited to attend the party.

The homeowners addressed the crowd and told how their Habitat houses had changed their lives. Greater self-esteem, more family togetherness, better school performance, less exposure to drugs . . . . As I listened to these stories, I realized it was the "sign" I had been seeking.

It was a Christmas I will always remember; the memory of it gives me the incentive to carry on.

Calvin & Ossia Whitehead

Our most memorable Christmas began in the Year of Our Lord 1976 when Millard Fuller started Habitat for Humanity.

Christmas 1988 brought a new belief in ourselves. It was a wonderful feeling when we moved into our new Habitat house with our two daughters and two sons.

We had lived in a run-down place before. Now we had new FAUCETS—everything—NEW. It was a new beginning for the Whitehead family.

We could relate to each other better. We celebrated the birthdays of new grandchildren. We celebrated the ownership of a home for our family.

And most of all we have a Christmas view of knowing that Jesus can bless, and that his blessings, through many volunteers, have helped us to write some of the memorable moments of the Georgians who remember Christmas.

ILLUSTRATION BY LINDA MITCHELL

Louise Arnold

I was born on Tye Street in Cabbagetown. Can you imagine the joy in our family when we were told we were getting a Habitat house on Tye Street? Incredible!

At that time I was living in three rooms with my children. My son Keith slept in the kitchen. My son Steven slept on the couch. My daughter Donna slept with me in our bed.

We worked with the wonderful Habitat volunteers and staff building our house. And on December 2, 1988, we moved into our new home.

Christmas that year was our best Christmas ever. We thank everyone who helped to make this possible!

ILLUSTRATION BY BETSY KOOLS

Frances Grimes

This will be our first Christmas in our new Habitat house.

For a long time we paid rent for an apartment and we were getting nowhere.

Now we are in a new house and it costs less than the apartment.

We are so thankful to be in a house that will be ours someday. We are going to work hard to keep it.

ILLUSTRATION BY ANNEKE BARLOW

Terina & Favous Horton

The best Christmas I can remember is waking up in my brand-new Habitat house.

I mean, it was unbelievable how one can come from a one-bedroom apartment in Carver Homes housing project to a lovely three-bedroom house. A house that we can call our own. It was the Christmas of 1990.

The best Christmas was seeing my children come out of their own bedrooms, walking down that hall to our brand-new living room filled with all that new furniture and toys. Just seeing the look on their faces made me want to jump for joy.

I just praise God and give Him all the glory because He is the one who made it possible for us to wake up in our own house (through Him anything is possible). Along with my husband, Favous, I thank Habitat and their workers for all their kindness and generosity they have shown to us.

Willie Pittman

At this time of the year all I can think of is how thankful I am to the Habitat crew and volunteers.

I was born in Mississippi and lived there twenty-two years. I remember my Christmas present when I was a young boy. Six oranges, about the same number of apples, a bag of walnuts, and maybe a stick of peppermint candy.

Now I am thankful that we have a Habitat house and I can get some Christmas presents for my child.

Tanyon Parker

On Christmas morning in 1988 I remember my children getting up and seeing the living room decorated—and their toys. My daughters were three and six, and my son sixteen.

This was our first Christmas in our new Habitat house.

And right after Christmas, we gave a wedding reception and barbecue outside in the cold. And we had a chance to show everybody our new home.

Shimeik Gordon

The First White Christmas Tree

The children have always wanted a big white Christmas tree. But we always lived in a small apartment and only had room for a small tree.

But now that we're in our Habitat house we have a beautiful place to put the tree. So we went out a few days before Thanksgiving and picked out a big white Christmas tree.

My daughters Shinika (ten) and Linda (seven) were so excited. They couldn't wait to decorate the tree. So we put it up the night before Thanksgiving. The children helped to place the blue and gold ornaments. And the white and blue lights. And then we sang some songs.

Now they look at the beautiful tree every night before they go to bed. And we all know that this is going to be our best Christmas ever.

Jackie Gray

In 1988 we had our first Christmas in our new Habitat house. It was built during the Jimmy Carter Work Camp in June of that year.

We had a big Christmas tree, which we decorated together. We had a big dinner, and lots of gifts. We took pictures—it was the best.

It's so peaceful in our new house. There's privacy; nobody beats on the walls like in our old apartment.

And guess who stopped by to say hello a month ago? Jimmy Carter, who helped build our house. Wasn't that nice of him to do that!

ILLUSTRATION BY LEROY SCOTT

Sheila Mason

Our first Christmas in our new Habitat house was a delight. It was filled with happiness and joy.

There were cakes and pies and flowers. And music—singing Christmas songs. And the decorated cedar tree. And opening presents with the family.

There was a real sharing of love within our family.

Sharon Collins

Who would think that a phone call could bring so much joy? Just ten days before Christmas in 1988 Tom Chapel called to tell me the junior high youth group from St. Luke's Church was giving a party for me and my family. It was to be at our new Habitat house. I argued over the phone that it must be a mistake, I didn't have a house. But it was true! I was to pick up the keys to my new home a few days later.

This was the year we all were out to help someone. My son Derek helped me deliver baskets to homes for the YMCA. My son Corey was in a play put on by South Atlanta Child Care—the money went to homeless children.

When someone asked, "What did you get for Christmas," I could only say, "a NEW HOUSE!"

Thanks to God, Habitat, St. Luke's and everyone who helped on the house.

ILLUSTRATION BY SUSAN JOSS

Kinyatah Heath

My mother, Juliette Rockmore, says I can tell what is special about Christmas—and it's singing!

Like "Rudolph the Red-Nosed Reindeer." And "Deck the Halls." And "Jingle Bells."

And I know "Joy to the World." And I know "Jingle Bells."

I like to sing!

Rosa Fowler

My daughter Kimberly, who is twelve years old, says that our Habitat house is truly a dream house. We love it. We praise God for it.

Kimberly's poem won a Golden Poet 1991 Award from the World of Poetry in Sacramento, California.

Dreamland

Dreamland seems to be a wonderful place.
There are rainbows and clouds filled with lace.
People are always looking around
But no one ever seems to look down.
Dreamland is for you and me
So come on down and you will see.
Dreamland is a place of dreams,
It's like a place you've never seen.
Dreamland only comes at night
So when you dream don't have a fright.

Good night!

ILLUSTRATION BY LINDA MITCHELL

Priscilla Knight

We have been in our Habitat house for a year and a half and it has been a big change. There has been a big improvement in our lives.

I was uneasy about raising my two children in a strongly drug-infested environment, but Habitat has changed this. I know there are drugs everywhere, but I feel safer in my new environment.

Habitat has been a big help to me and my family, not only in building me a home but also in my time of need. Last year I lost my nephew in a shooting. Habitat was there when I needed them.

I thank Habitat for all they have done for me. And my son, William, has written down his thoughts:

This House

As the Holiday Season comes around again, I thank the Lord for my health, for my family's health, and I thank the Lord for this house. This house that I have spent a year and a half in. This house that I helped build from the ground up. This house where I have spent a wonderful Thanksgiving, Christmas, New Year, Easter, and eighteenth birthday. This house—my house—now who should I thank for that? My mother Priscilla Knight, the Lord, and, most of all, Habitat.

Marie Billings

Christmas isn't just when you get toys and presents. It's very important to remember that Christmas is the birthday of Jesus Christ.

It's a time for giving. And the Habitat people gave so much, so that we could have a home.

I want to say thank you. And I hope all of you have a happy and jolly Christmas.

ILLUSTRATION BY BILL THOMPSON

The Habitat Story

For the past eighteen years Larry has worked from 11 at night until 8 in the morning restocking shelves at the local supermarket.

Now it's 8:30 Saturday morning. Larry is probably at home having breakfast, right? Or already in bed resting his weary bones, right?

Wait a minute! Isn't that Larry hammering nails and building his dream house in Cabbagetown? And isn't that his wife and one of their sons carrying lumber and nails from the truck to the house?

And who are those twenty other people helping Larry and his family to build a house? Let's ask them.

" 'Scuse me, sir. What company is building this house?"

"Habitat. Volunteers. I'm a student at Emory U. during the week."

"Why are you here today?"

"Too many working people in Atlanta living in sub-standard housing. Can't afford their own home. Habitat makes it possible."

"Is that a fact? Young lady with the hammer, what do you do?"

"Cashier at the drug store on Boulevard Drive. I live across the street."

"Why Habitat?"

"Partnership between black and white. Rich and poor. It works."

"If you say so. Sir, what do you do besides fit windows into those walls?"

"Airline pilot."

"Why this?"

"A sense of accomplishment. You see the results of your efforts. We'll be under roof by 3 P.M. today."

"I'll believe that when I see it. Pardon me, Miss. Isn't that roof truss a little heavy for you? What do you do during the week?"

"Homemaker in Dunwoody. Two teen-age sons. This roof truss is a piece of cake."

"Why Habitat?"

"Home ownership brings self-esteem. Incentive to work. Families stay together. Some homeowners even tell us their kids are more likely to stay in school."

"Makes sense, I guess. Say mister, can you talk to me from that ladder and tell me what you do during the week?"

"Construction worker. Highway Department."

"Why do you do this on Saturday?"

"Habitat built a home for me in Edgewood. Just returning the favor. Helping people help themselves."

"Yeah, I can see that. Wow, young lady, did you bring this table full of sandwiches, potato salad and brownies? And why?"

"Bible says we should open our hand and our heart to our poor brother. Here, put these three gallons of tea at the far end of the table. Now ring that dinner bell and stand back or you'll get trampled."

That's it! That's Habitat. *Partnership.* Rich and poor. Black and white. Various educational backgrounds. Various religious denominations. From all parts of the city. *All working together* to build decent houses for God's people in need.

Opportunities

... at Habitat for Humanity in Atlanta:

DONATE

If you would like to help us build affordable housing for low-income families, please send a check to:

Habitat for Humanity in Atlanta
1125 Seaboard Avenue, NE
Atlanta, Georgia 30307

All donations are tax deductible.

VOLUNTEER

If you would like to volunteer, we have need for your help in property acquisition, family selection, family relations, public relations, office work, and special events. Please call us at:

Habitat for Humanity in Atlanta
404/223 - 5180.

Thank You!

Habitat for Humanity
in Atlanta
Board of Directors

Tom Chapel, President
Bruce Gunter, Vice-President
Lynn Merrill, Vice-President
Lige Moore, Vice-President

Bill Adams
Wayne Angel
Daisy Bailey
Carolyn Baldwin
Judy Clements
Pete Daniel
Bill & Eve Earnest
Adrienne Findley
Linda Gabbard
Bob Geiger
Jackie Goodman
Al Griffin
Mary Jane Heussner
Willie Hinton
Shirley Kilgore

Al Kirkpatrick
Mary Line
W. Andrew McKenna
Don Millen
Amy Nicholson
Bill Pendleton
Alexandra Pieper-Jones
Jeanne Shorthouse
Jayne Sizer
Gene Stelten
Van Dyke Walker, Jr.
Janis Ware
Harriette D. Watkins
Phillip R. White
Roderick R. White

Habitat for Humanity in Atlanta Advisory Council

Ronald W. Allen
Bill Campbell
Johnnetta Cole
Dr. W. Frank Harrington
Jimmy Hewell
Maynard Jackson
Frank C. Jones
Archbishop James Lyke
Joseph G. Martin, Jr.
Dr. Joseph Roberts
Herman J. Russell
B. Franklin Skinner
Deen Day Smith
Susan W. Wieland

Staff

Larry Arney, Executive Director
Mary Alice Alexander, Development Director
Brendan Breault, Office Manager
Kore Thompson, Volunteer Coordinator
Gilbert Nicholson, Construction Supervisor
Tom Robinson, House Leader
Paul Locascio, House Leader
Jeanne Shorthouse, House Leader
Francis Boswell, House Leader
Scott Reale, House Leader
Pat McGauley, House Leader
Randy Lane, House Leader